I0487538

Copyright Notice

© 2004 by Al Kernek

Edition 2; August 2004

TABLE OF CONTENTS

LIST OF TABLES

LIST OF FIGURES

1. WHAT THIS BOOK WILL TELL YOU

This book is designed specifically for agents and brokers in the residential real estate business, and those servicing this industry. It provides a concise guide, demonstrating how to implement e-mail newsletter campaigns that best fit your time, wallet, resources and expertise.

Everyone can have a professional looking e-mail newsletter (or Website for that matter). You do not have to be a technical guru to accomplish this. Regardless of your technical proficiency, there is a course of action outlined here for you. This book gives you the knowledge and identifies the tools that allow you to create a strategy compatible with your unique circumstances.

Hundreds of hours of research and years of experience have gone into creating the information here for your benefit. The goal is to help you derive a personal roadmap for launching your own e-mail newsletter. Rather than taking a shot in the dark, readers will gain a clear understanding of what is involved and what resources are available to assist them. Exhaustive research has distilled a myriad of confusing data down to the essential information, tools and applications that best serve the real estate community in this endeavor.

Readers will save hundreds of dollars and countless hours of research. The research has been done for you. Free software that can be downloaded off the Web is identified, as are reputable commercial packages and outsource vendors. The "do's" and "don'ts" of electronic newsletter publishing are covered. Why and how to create your own professional Website for under $10 monthly is explained.

Those who dive into creating a newsletter without first understanding the scope of the project, or what options are available, often suffer through a frustrating and expensive experience. You will learn how to avoid the pitfalls doom a newsletter to failure. You will learn how to create and manage e-mail newsletter marketing campaigns that boost your earnings while requiring little ongoing effort or expense.

People who are in the real estate business are cost-conscious. While you want an effective marketing campaign that helps your sales, you don't want it to spend a lot on it –in some cases, nothing at all - or have it consume too much of your precious time. That is why emphasis here is placed on identifying free or inexpensive solutions that both enhance your productivity and will help your newsletter be successful.

In here, you will find simple explanations of what can be complex subjects. Charts, tables and summaries reduce a plethora of data down to just the essential elements you need to understand. This approach lets you easily identify solutions that best fit your needs.

Chapter 1: What This Book Will Tell You

Each chapter builds on the previous, culminating in a process guaranteed to yield a strategy that works best for you. When you complete this book, you will have a straightforward roadmap of how best to proceed, an understanding of the costs (if any) involved, and an idea of how you can upgrade initial efforts in the future.

The book begins by defining the nature of an e-mail newsletter, explaining its content and immense benefits. It also tells you how to avoid pitfalls, like being accused of "spamming."

For the economy-minded, the book explains how you can use your own PC, along with Microsoft Outlook, Word and free Web downloads to create attractive, interesting e-mail newsletters that can be regularly sent to your customers, prospects or partners. We ultimately graduate to more sophisticated tools and outsource services. In-between, it shows you a variety of options for adding low-cost capabilities to dramatically enhance the success of your e-mail newsletter campaigns.

You will learn how to automate newsletter processes for ongoing management and prospecting. For those with (or contemplating) a Website, you will learn how to leverage newsletters to drive traffic to your website. And if you don't have a Website, you will learn why you should consider this step and what low-cost, easily-implemented options are open to you.

Written in plain English for non-techies, with plenty of examples and buyer comparison charts, the book is intended to pinpoint solutions that best satisfy your unique goals and budget. Specifically, you will learn how to:

- Create interesting, attractive e-mail newsletters.
- Prepare newsletter content, and where to find free articles and other information sources.
- Where to get free newsletter templates.
- Find free resources that will help you design your newsletter.
- Gather e-mail addresses and grow your prospect base.
- Promote your persona so that your name and face become synonymous with the local real estate market.
- Avoid legal and market pitfalls when creating and sending e-mail newsletters.
- Minimize the cost of creating and managing newsletter campaigns by using your own PC, Microsoft Word and Outlook, and free Web downloads.
- Become more effective by spending just a little money to get integrated commercial tools that magnify your productivity.
- Easily create or link to a Website and why you should consider this.
- Create inexpensive Websites with substantial benefits.
- Employ easily-implemented tools that automatically manage and promote your e-mail newsletter.
- Engage "worry free" outsource services that automatically send personalized newsletters to your clients.

- Develop a strategy that works best for you, identify specific approaches and costs (if any) upfront.

Throughout this process, the book provides interactive links to a multitude of Websites where additional information or suggested software can be found. Free e-mail newsletter templates, wizards, content sources and marketing tools that can be used to your advantage are also identified.

Anyone in the real estate community contemplating an e-mail newsletter will benefit immensely from the contents of this book. Readers will gain exactly the degree of knowledge necessary to be successful. With the information learned here, you will avoid common pitfalls and enjoy a streamlined implementation. You will also do this at less expense than those who stumble into launching a newsletter. Unlike some horror stories you may have heard, you will know where you are going, how to get there, and how to achieve this within your personal budget.

Assumptions about You, the Reader

You do not have to be a "techie" to benefit from this book. Anyone who has used a personal computer (PC) and Microsoft Office products will be able to easily grasp the material presented herein. Creating and using effective e-mail newsletters is not a difficult undertaking if you understand the essentials of any word-processing and e-mail application.

For the purposes of this book, it is assumed that you, the reader, own or have access to a PC or Macintosh, have a basic familiarity with Microsoft Windows[1] (operating software), Word (word processing) and Outlook (e-mail), and are capable of interfacing to the Internet and navigating Websites. The processes outlined in this book can also be applied to alternative tools, such as Word Perfect and Eudora e-mail, but you will have to make the technical translation yourself to accomplish that. Regardless of what PC mechanisms are employed, the concepts and information contained herein will provide you with an understanding of how to approach, create and manage e-mail newsletters as a powerful marketing tool.

It is assumed that you are an experienced PC user, who knows how to use a mouse to select, cut and paste documents, photos, logos, text and Website links. Within Word, you should be comfortable with:

- The creation, modification and manipulation of tables and columns.
- Inserting objects (photos, etc.) into Word documents.
- Selecting, copying and pasting objects and text.
- How to modify the font and appearance of text.
- How to create and manipulate tables.

---

[1] Windows 98 or higher is strongly recommended. Ideally, you should have Office XP (which requires Windows XP....funny how Microsoft keeps making you buy both to get the full benefit of upgrades) to easily follow the instructions that are given in this book. However, the same operations can be performed in previous Office versions with minor changes in the procedure.

If you can do these things, you can create impressive e-mail newsletters that will dramatically enhance your marketing effectiveness. A cursory review of these operations is included, but it is suggested that readers consult Microsoft Word Help for detailed instructions.

It is also assumed that you have not been living in a cave or distant planet for the last five years and that you are aware of, have seen and probably read an e-mail newsletter. But just in case, we cover that subject too.

Lastly, it is assumed that you are willing to try something new, something that requires effort on your part to be successful. You must be personally motivated to master e-mail newsletters and willing to learn the steps involved in their preparation. After all, the more effective you become in using your newsletter as a marketing tool, the more money you will ultimately put into your pocket.

Conventions

To make instructions easy to follow throughout the book, standard nomenclature is followed:

- Embedded hyperlinks (i.e., active links to a Website page) are displayed in blue. You can go directly to the referenced Website or Page simply by clicking on the link. For example, by placing your cursor on http://www.realtor.org/rodesign.nsf/pages/HomePage?OpenDocument and clicking your mouse, your Internet browser is automatically launched to open the home page of the Realtor Website.

  Now, Websites are notorious about changing the addresses for embedded Webpages. So if the hyperlink in this book does not work, simply copy the portion of the link that goes up to the ".com," ".net." or ".org" part into your Internet browser address box (at the top of the browser) to get to the main Website page. In the above example, you would enter www.realtor.org. Once there, hunt for the referenced product or service on the main Website page. Most Websites have a "search" box where you can enter the name of the product or service to find its embedded Webpage. Click on the appropriate links returned by the search engine and it will take you the desired Webpage where you can learn more about the product or service and how to purchase or download it.

- Application instructions are presented in a consistent (italicized) manner that is easy to follow. The Microsoft Word program instructions, *Edit/Select All* followed by *Edit/Copy*, for example, direct you to complete this operation by first clicking on the Edit menu at the top of your Word or Outlook screen (which causes a roll-down menu to appear) and then clicking on "Select All" (which highlights everything in your open document). Then, click on "Copy" under the Edit roll-down menu to place the selected material on the Microsoft Clipboard for subsequent pasting into a new document (*Edit/Paste*). These operations can also be accessed by right-clicking your mouse. Any questions you may have about Word operations can be answered by clicking on "Help" at the top of the Word screen and following the instructions given to you there.

- "Select" also means to highlight a photo, logo or text using your mouse cursor. Selecting text usually involves clicking at the start of the targeted text string and then dragging your mouse across the desired text. You can also select rows, columns and cells within a table. Linked or embedded objects (e.g., photos, graphics, or charts) can be selected for copy/paste operations as well. Again, please refer to Word or Outlook Help if you have any questions about how to perform these operations.

  For shortcut purposes, you can select text or a graphic object (e.g., a photos or logo), then click the right button on your mouse to access a pop-up menu which allows you to quickly take a subsequent action (such as *Copy*) involving the selected material.

The term "Grab" is used in conjunction with selecting a line or border to perform some action while holding down the left mouse key. For example "Grab the table border and expand the table width as necessary to fill your screen" is an instruction that results in a wider table by dynamically using your mouse to expand the table width to the desired proportions.

2. WHAT IS AN E-MAIL NEWSLETTER?

E-mail newsletters are similar to bulk mail. However, they are delivered over the Internet directly to the intended reader. This is a much more effective and lower-cost means of reaching prospects than sending postcards or brochures through "snail mail," or the U.S. Postal system. An e-mail newsletter is the ideal vehicle to stay in touch with customers and prospective clients.

Think of the e-mail newsletters you receive now. You may get one or more investment newsletters from SmartMoney.com, Morningstar or the Motley Fool. Maybe you get a daily newsletter summarizing the results of today's sports events or an update on travel bargains. Perhaps information about a weekend sale at Mervyns, Walmart, or Victoria Secrets welcomes you when you turn on your computer in the morning. You may get a newsletter from a club or organization (e.g., your state Realtor Association) or an interesting Website where you have requested to be kept informed. E-mail newsletters now permeate our lives and are accepted as a valuable, timely means of delivering useful information. In the world of commerce, for instance, e-mail newsletters are fast becoming a dominant form of communication between businesses and prospective buyers, whether it's goods, services or information that is being sold.

Much like printed newsletters or daily newspapers, real estate e-mail newsletters contain information of interest to the targeted reader. For residential sales, this may be information on current mortgage rates, price trends in the local area or even home repair tips. Your goal in preparing an e-mail newsletter is to capture a reader's attention when they first open it. Providing interesting, useful information is critical to building your newsletter circulation. The reaction you want from your readers is, "Yea, this is good stuff." If you can achieve that, then you've opened the door to direct delivery of marketing messages into the homes and businesses that represent your customers.

What's Unique about E-Mail Newsletters?

While e-mail newsletters can become part of your arsenal to maintain a market presence, they differ from standard newspapers, flyers and brochures in one important aspect: information content is not the ultimate purpose of e-mail newsletters. Because of the interactive qualities of the Internet, e-mail newsletters are powerful marketing tools. In addition to strengthening a relationship with a client, the goal of an e-mail newsletter is to motivate a reader to take some action WHEN they read it. This may be to:

- Subscribe to your newsletter (if it was forwarded to them).
- Visit your Website to see your listings or programs.
- Respond to a promotional offer.
- Buy something.
- Forward your e-mail to a friend, co-worker or relative who they know is interested in buying or selling a residence.
- Visit you at a local trade show booth.
- Sign up for an event, such as a real estate seminar for potential buyers.
- Request more information on a subject.
- Contact you directly for advice, etc.

Hence, your newsletter should be constructed with these objectives in mind. Ask yourself, "What would I like the reader to do when they digest my newsletter, and how can I get them to do that?"

Beware of Spamming

The secret behind successful e-mail newsletters is that the recipient has requested (or "opted-in") that the newsletter be sent to him or her by either subscribing to it or indicating a desire to receive online information of this nature. Readers are also assured that their privacy is protected and are given the option of easily unsubscribing to the newsletter.

"Spam" is unwanted or unsolicited e-mail. Who hasn't received an e-mail advertisement for Viagra, free credit repair, or life insurance? Spammers have tools called "spiders" that craw through the Internet and gleam e-mail addresses off Websites. They package these into huge mail lists and broadcast advertisements around the world. Spam turns people off!

Spam costs consumers millions of dollars annually, reduces work productivity and endangers legitimate Internet marketing. Recognizing this impact, Congress has passed legislation in an attempt to curtail spamming:

> *CAN-SPAM, also known as Controlling the Assault of Non-Solicited Pornography and Marketing Act of 2003, requires that commercial e-mail carry an opt-out option so recipients can tell a sender to stop. The e-mail also must feature a real-life address so the sender can be contacted. Spammers who violate the law could be hit with thousands of dollars in fines or even jail time[2].*

But the major spammers are offshore companies whose Return addresses and "opt-out" procedures rarely work.

YOU DO NOT WANT TO BE LABELED AS A SPAMMER! It alienates your market, and that is not a good way to do business. In some cases, the intended reader will even bad-mouth you to his friends, co-workers and relatives.....sort of like "viral marketing" in reverse. Worse, anti-spam software used by Internet Service Providers and individual homeowners could be invoked to blacklist all your e-mails! In short, spamming your marketplace can have BAD consequences.

To avoid being labeled a spammer, follow these simple rules:

- **Always get permission before sending an e-mail newsletter**. Permission must be obtained by asking a customer or subscriber to sign up for your newsletter and ideally sending a confirming e-mail when they do so. Many companies now require new subscribers to "double opt-in" by clicking on an embedded link in the confirmation e-mail, such as "Click here to confirm your subscription," which records that the subscriber has confirmed that he/she wants to receive the newsletter. Confirmations of this nature are maintained with the subscriber's computer-based record in case an accusation of spamming is levied against the company in the future. If you do not use a "double opt-in" method, it is recommended that you at least maintain a copy of the new subscriber's e-mail or response which initially signed them up for your newsletter.

  Permission is also implied if you purchase an "opt-in" e-mail list wherein the recipients have previously requested information of the nature contained in your newsletter – in this case, information about residential real estate. When you use an opt-in list, it is suggested that you include a statement at the beginning or end of the newsletter similar to: "This e-mail newsletter is being sent to you because you previously granted permission to receive information of this nature. If you do not wish to receive future newsletters, please....."

- **Always provide a workable means for recipients to remove themselves from your subscription list**. When you receive a "remove" request, make sure you comply within 48 hours. Ideally, send the requester an e-mail confirming his/her removal.

---

[2] With anti-spam law in effect, companies work to foil junk e-mail; USA Today; 2/24/04.

3. WHY USE E-MAIL NEWSLETTERS?

Today, e-mail newsletters are used extensively in corporate America to maintain contact with customers, sell products online, offer special promotions, and to recruit new customers. They have proven to be extremely cost-effective in this endeavor.

While there is no doubt that today's real estate professionals should be using e-mail newsletters to promote themselves to their markets, most have not yet employed this inexpensive mechanism. Why? There are many reasons, from lack of knowledge to just not knowing how to get started. And there are a bewildering array of choices and issues when you start to research the subject. Many in the real estate industry simply give up and conclude that the whole subject of e-mail newsletters is just too technical to tackle.

Nonsense! Companies big and small have trail-blazed this new medium and an assortment of easy-to-use tools are now at your disposal. E-mail newsletters are neither difficult to prepare nor manage....if you understand how to approach them. Realtors, lenders, escrow and title companies and appraisers who have embraced e-mail newsletters as the cornerstone of their marketing strategy are enjoying tremendous upswings in revenue and productivity.

How would you like to double or triple your income over the next twelve months? Wouldn't it be nice to have people contact you to represent them in the purchase or sale of a home? Wouldn't you enjoy having prospects taking the initiative to seek you out for assistance rather than pounding the pavement to find them? Wouldn't it be great to have your clients referring you to their neighbors, co-workers, friends and families as the "real estate expert" they should engage? Implementing a sustained, ongoing e-mail newsletter campaign can make these desires a reality!

> **65% of the U.S. population uses the Internet.**
> Barron's.

Location, location, location" may be the primary factor in determining the market value of a residence, but a steady, continuing "presence" in the marketplace is essential to retaining real estate customers and capturing new ones.

Using regularly-scheduled e-mail newsletters to keep in contact with customers and prospects has proven to be an excellent means of "touching" clients and generating new business at a very low cost. In the everyday world of real estate, there is no better means of creating new business than by sending informative newsletters. E-mail newsletters keep your name and face in front of your market so that when people decide to sell – or buy – a home, they will naturally think of you as the expert to engage for their transaction. After all, you will be the one whose image has come into their home or office on a regular basis,

> **According to the N.A.R., 70% of all transactions were initiated from the internet.**

bestowing knowledge and a sense of expertise. Your name will be instilled in their minds as the most likely person to turn to when they make one of the most important decisions in their life – whom to trust with selling their home or buying a new one (or both!).

The same is true for organizations servicing the residential real estate industry. E-mail newsletters are an opportunity to provide Realtors with valuable information, enhancing their awareness of industry issues and providing updates about how their clients can benefit from your latest offerings. Newsletters are an excellent means of supporting Realtors with critical information necessary to become more effective in closing new sales. Given everyone's busy schedule, it is difficult to stay current on new regulations, recently introduced programs and market trends. A monthly newsletter that offers useful information about industry developments is a blessing. Periodic communications from lenders, escrow and title companies, or appraisers can assist Realtors in understanding important subjects, such as comprehending what programs are available for different types of clients, the impact of new regulations, and generally handling the concerns of buyers and sellers alike. Successful Realtors need strong business partnerships, and e-mail newsletters are a powerful means of cultivating these relationships.

How Will I Benefit?

A major challenge in any business is gaining awareness of your company, products or services among existing and potential customers. This is the first step in earning their trust. If you consistently communicate your expertise to prospects and illustrate how this can benefit them, then you are more likely to gain their business.

It is axiomatic in business that existing or past customers should never be neglected. Maintaining a strong relationship with your customer and partner base is a prerequisite to earning future business. Moreover, astute business people know that satisfied clients are an excellent source for referral business.

This is especially true in real estate. Nothing builds a strong relationship with clients, prospects or partners like maintaining a consistent dialogue. Realtors do this now by tried and true farming methods - delivering flyers, mailing post cards, joining local clubs and organizations to meet people or knocking on doors to introduce themselves. Companies involved in the sales process - lenders, and title and escrow companies - may speak at a weekly brokerage meeting or bring donuts by the office. Essentially, we in the real estate industry use a variety of methods to "drip, drip, drip" messages to its markets in an attempt to strengthen important relationships. Realtors are pros at this – they want their name and face to immediately come to mind when a homeowner decides to sell or someone asks, "Who can help me to find and buy a home?"

For all those involved in the real estate buying and selling process, e-mail newsletters are another arrow in your quiver, but one that is much more potent than any you have used before. By consistently delivering an e-mail newsletter to your customers and partners, you will strengthen your relationships and increase the likelihood of capturing future transactions.

E-mail newsletters take on a life of their own too. If they are interesting, they are more likely to get passed around, resulting in a kind of virtual marketing program. In fact, the latest term for this is "viral marketing." Often, recipients will save interesting e-mails to an Outlook folder for future reference (like when they decide to sell their home!). Since e-mails are easily and frequently forwarded, you never know where copies of your newsletter are going to end up. For you, this represents a tremendous opportunity to get your name and face in front of prospective clients.

Newsletters are also a vehicle for gathering new e-mail addresses and growing your list of prospects. If you have a Website, e-mail newsletters are very effective in driving readers to your site where they can learn more about you, your listings and the services your company offers to assist them in selling or buying a home.

Imagine being contacted by unknown sellers or buyers who received your forwarded newsletter just when they were perusing the Yellow Pages for local Realtors! Lenders – don't be surprised if a Realtor calls you because they saved a newsletter explaining a new "first time buyer" program that is just perfect for their clients. Appraisers – be ready to respond to lenders and Realtors who need a quick appraisal, and decided to engage your services because of those consistent newsletters you've been sending them offering a 24-hour turnaround program or free upfront value assessments based on comps.

More Bang for Your Buck

E-mail newsletters are extremely cost-effective tools that significantly enhance your productivity. The typical cost of producing a direct mail piece and accompanying postage is typically between $.35 and $.50, depending on the volume. Flyers and brochures are expensive too and require a lot walking and time to distribute. Aside from "sweat equity," basic e-mail newsletters cost nothing to produce and send. And once implemented, you will be able to devote your time to more productive activities than licking stamps or knocking on doors.

Interesting e-mail newsletters are much more likely to be read than a flyer or direct mail piece. One reputable source indicates that recipients are ten times more likely to read and respond to an e-mail newsletter compared to an advertisement received by regular mail. The reason is that newsletter readers have requested its delivery whereas bulk mail is typically viewed as an intrusion. When sending an e-mail newsletter to a willing subscriber list, industry figures show a 60-to-75 percent opening rate and "click through" rates up to ten percent on enclosed links. This compares to a typical one-to-two percent response rate from more expensive direct mail campaigns.

Chapter 3: Why Use E-Mail Newsletters?

If you have a PC (or Mac), you can quickly learn how to easily create attractive, interesting e-mail newsletters that get read and lead to an ever-growing prospect list. And the best part is that, having had the fine sense to purchase this book, you can get started today at no cost to yourself!

4. NEWSLETTER FORMAT AND CONTENT

Before we address how to create newsletters, let's take a moment to examine their content and structure. There are certain elements that all newsletters should contain. For ease of reading and navigation, newsletters should be structured in certain fashions. An understanding of these factors makes the actual preparation of a newsletter much easier.

This chapter will help you to visualize the content and structure of a newsletter. It educates you on the various formats of newsletters. The objective is to give you a "forest-level" view of newsletters before drilling down to the tree level in the next chapter. When you complete this chapter, you will understand what type of content should be placed in your newsletter, as well as the different types of newsletters you can employ in a marketing campaign. You will also exit this chapter with some thoughts about how you can layout your own newsletter.

Types of E-Mail Newsletters

There are many types of e-mail newsletters in use today, but rather than overwhelm you with technical jargon, we will only focus on the two recommended for Realtors. These are a simple, text-based newsletter and one that contains colorful graphics. As we progress in this book, you need to decide which type best suits your level of expertise, matches the effort you wish to put into creating your newsletter, and satisfies your personal budget for this project:

Format	Pros	Cons
Text-Oriented Newsletter: Essentially a "black and white" newsletter, it consists of text only, possibly supplemented with your e-mail address and links to your Website. The entire content of the newsletter can be presented within the newsletter itself, in which case the reader is able to digest embedded articles simply by scrolling down through the e-mail. Alternatively, article summaries can be included, supplemented by a link to your Website for the full story.	Easier to prepare and ensures that all recipients can read the newsletter. Some people still do not have e-mail applications that allow graphics of HTML reception. Others do, but do not set it up to process graphical materials. Some Internet Service Providers, like AOL, have difficulties in processing some types of graphics for their e-mail application.	Not as attention-getting as colorful e-mail newsletters that include graphics. May be viewed as "old fashion" by your readers. Doesn't allow you to insert your brokerage logo or photo into the newsletter to reinforce your image as the source of provided information. Difficult to include "action" buttons to induce some behavior on the part of the reader (such as, "Click here to sign up for our contest").

Format	Pros	Cons
Graphically-Oriented Newsletter: Developed using Word or Web-oriented tools. Its structural layout consists of frames, columns or rows. Use of complementary shading, graphics, photos, colored fonts and links to external Websites is typical. Usually, only article lead-ins or summaries are included in the newsletter; readers must travel to a linked Website to get the full story.	More likely to capture attention from prospective clients. Allows more construction and content flexibility. You can include more materials in one mailing without the attendant risk of overwhelming the reader. Once on your Website, you can track readers' interest by analyzing where they click. Allows you to insert your photo and other graphics into the newsletter. Better format for including interactive "action" buttons (Graphical buttons that are clicked to launch a process. For example, the button might be titled, "Download Free Market Report")	Some clients may not have e-mail software that can process graphics or photos. Some may have this capability but are using incorrect settings. If links to external Websites are embedded, you must ensure that these remain functional.

Ideally, a graphically-oriented newsletter is suggested, as this has proven to be more effective in gaining attention and readership. Text-oriented newsletters were the first type implemented before e-mail applications became capable of processing images. While still used, this format is declining as all major e-mail software packages now include the capability to present graphical materials.

To cover all bases, however, many newsletter providers offer readers a choice when they register for a subscription – do you want text- or graphical-newsletter formats? Of course, this means preparing two types of e-mail newsletters. Certain commercial software applications and services, which you can purchase, automatically convert graphically-oriented e-mail newsletters into text-oriented newsletters after detecting the recipients e-mail settings.

But don't worry about that now. Rather, focus on which type of e-mail newsletter you would like to implement. Now let's take a look at the overall lay-out of both types.

Overview of Newsletter Structures

The structure of both types of newsletters is similar in content but much different in formatting. Text-oriented newsletters deliver the bare essentials, but lack attention-grabbing flair. In contrast, graphically-oriented newsletters entice reader with a variety of colors, layouts and interactive links.

Text-Oriented Newsletters are Easy to Prepare

A text-oriented newsletter is pretty simple in nature, but usually contains these elements:

```
Greeting and Title
*******************************************************************
Your Contact Information (Name, Phone, Website Address, and E-
mail Address)
*******************************************************************
In This Issue (List Story Titles)
*******************************************************************
Story #1 (Headline and Text; Possible Links to Website)
*******************************************************************
Story #2 (Headline and Text; Possible Links to Website)
*******************************************************************
.
.
.
*******************************************************************
Story #N (Headline and Text; Possible Website URLs)
*******************************************************************
Action Lines (Headline and Text with possible URL for Website)
*******************************************************************
Subscription and "Removal" Information
*******************************************************************
```

Here is an example of how these elements might be appear in a text-oriented e-mail newsletter:

```
Welcome to your April 2004 Edition of the ABC Realty Newsletter!
* * * * * * * * * * * * * * * * * * * * * * * * * * * * * * * * * * * * * * * * * * * * * *
This newsletter is brought to you by Jane Smith, your certified Realtor
at ABC Realty.

Phone: 858-333-1221   E-Mail: jsmith@abcrealty.com, www.abcrealty.com

Serving the real estate needs of this community for 10 years.
* * * * * * * * * * * * * * * * * * * * * * * * * * * * * * * * * * * * * * * * * * * * * *
In This Issue:

* Value of Local Homes Continue to Rise
* Mortgage Rates to Stay Low
* It's a Seller's Market!

Scroll down for stories
```

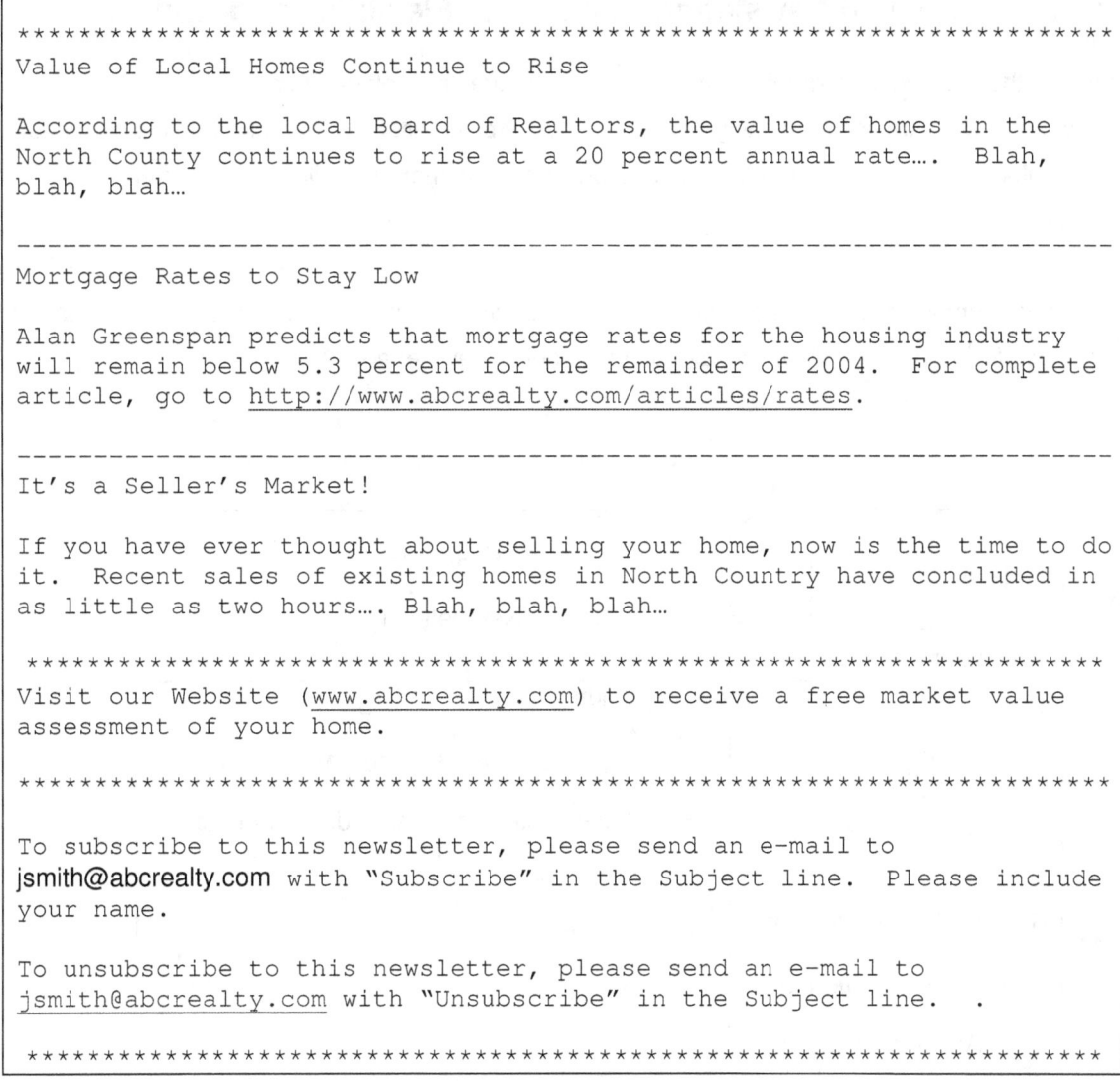

```
*************************************************************
Value of Local Homes Continue to Rise

According to the local Board of Realtors, the value of homes in the
North County continues to rise at a 20 percent annual rate…. Blah,
blah, blah…


-------------------------------------------------------------
Mortgage Rates to Stay Low

Alan Greenspan predicts that mortgage rates for the housing industry
will remain below 5.3 percent for the remainder of 2004. For complete
article, go to http://www.abcrealty.com/articles/rates.


-------------------------------------------------------------
It's a Seller's Market!

If you have ever thought about selling your home, now is the time to do
it. Recent sales of existing homes in North Country have concluded in
as little as two hours…. Blah, blah, blah…

*************************************************************
Visit our Website (www.abcrealty.com) to receive a free market value
assessment of your home.

*************************************************************

To subscribe to this newsletter, please send an e-mail to
jsmith@abcrealty.com with "Subscribe" in the Subject line. Please include
your name.

To unsubscribe to this newsletter, please send an e-mail to
jsmith@abcrealty.com with "Unsubscribe" in the Subject line. .

*************************************************************
```

Notice that only plain text appears. In fact, text-oriented e-mail is formatted using just a few variables:

- Dashes or characters can be used to sectionalize a newsletter
- Embedded Website and e-mail links are spelled out and underlined as active links.
- Line Spaces have been used to offset information and provide visual aesthetics.

When creating a text-based e-mail newsletter, it is important to limit your line width to 65 characters or less. Otherwise, your newsletter will lose its formatting on a recipient's screen that is set up for a text-only display. Also, it is best to use a text editor, like Microsoft Notepad rather than Word. Be sure to hit the Return or Enter key at the end of each line (even if it's not the end of a sentence) to ensure proper formatting is displayed when a client opens your newsletter e-mail.

Graphically-Oriented Newsletters Have More Flexibility and Appeal

From an aesthetic standpoint, graphical newsletters with attractive colors and photos are more likely to get read. Certainly, they are easier to navigate. Moreover, by being assured that embedded e-mail addresses and hyperlinks will survive, graphical newsletters provide much more flexibility in the content and structuring of a newsletter.

A graphically-oriented newsletter is constructed by separating a page into "frames" or sections, each of which contains specific information. A typical lay-out for graphical newsletters is:

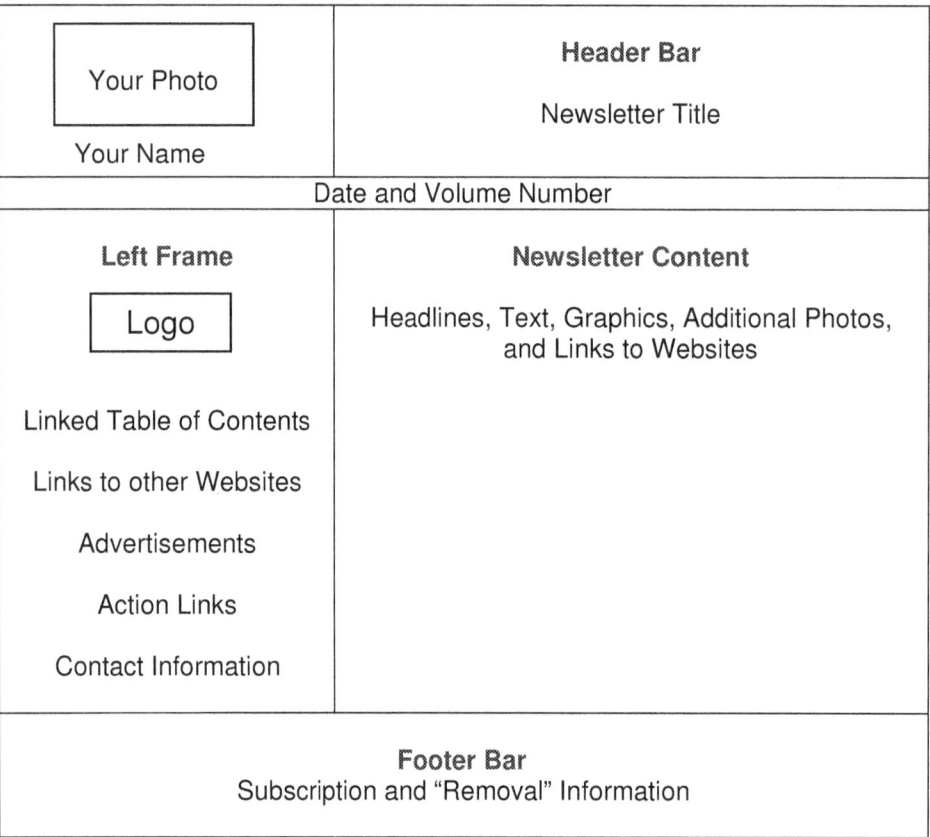

Referencing the next page, notice how the information presented in a graphical newsletter has a much stronger visual impact on the reader. Several things are apparent:

The use of colored frames (i.e., sections) and fonts, graphics (logo) and embedded photos with different fonts and sizes makes this a much more appealing newsletter than a text-oriented one. Graphical newsletters are more likely to grab a reader's attention and to be forwarded to friends, co-workers or relatives.

You can embed promotional information (such as the Featured Listing), something that cannot be done with text-oriented newsletters.

It's easier for the reader to quickly find what he/she is looking for and to navigate there with this format. "Action Links" in a side frame allow readers to be directed to specific Website locations where they can be induced to take actions beneficial to your purpose.

In the example on the next page, the black arrows demonstrate the internal links from the table of contents ("In This Issue") to the stories. This facilitates vertical scrolling and allows readers to quickly jump to an article of interest. To access the entire story, the reader must click on "more" which takes him to a Web page (or alternatively further down in the scrolling e-mail).

Action links allow the Realtor to promote his other listings by channeling the reader to a Website where these can be accessed. The second action link is designed to gain new prospects. Clicking there generates a "forwarding" e-mail in which the newsletter originator's e-mail address is already present on the "To" line. The "ABC Realty" logo in the left frame, the Realty Website address and even the Realtor's photo can all be hot links that when activated take the reader to a specific Web location. Of course, clicking on the Realtor's e-mail address will automatically launch a blank Outlook e-mail to the Realtor for the reader to use in constructing a message.

Take another look at this graphical example. Wouldn't you as a reader be intrigued by these articles? As a reader, you would probably also look at the Featured Listing and may even transfer to the Realtor's Web-based listings just to get an idea of the values in your area. The newsletter may contain a relevant article causing the reader to forward the e-mail to a friend. Or, the reader may think of someone who is house hunting and immediately forward the newsletter to them.

Imagine yourself receiving a newsletter like this on a monthly basis and answer the question, "Who am I going to think of when I want to sell my home? What Realtor consistently demonstrates competence to me, so that I feel comfortable referring my new co-worker to him/her?" That's the power of e-mail newsletters.

Your Local Real Estate Newsletter

Jane Doe, Realtor®

Volume 1, May 2003

ABC REALTORS

In This Issue:

Value of Local Homes Continue to Rise

It's a Seller's Market!

Featured Listing

Click Here to See All Our Listings

ABC Realtors
125 Elm Street
Suite 100
Anywhere, CA 92028

Phone:
(619) 555-0111

Fax:
(619) 555-0122

E-mail:
info@abcrealtors.com

We're on the Web!
www.abcrealtors.com

Value of Local Homes Continue to Rise

According to the San Diego Board of Realtors, the value of homes in the North County continue to rise at a 20 percent annual rate... more

It's a Seller's Market!

If you have ever thought about selling your home, now is the time to do it. Recent sales of existing homes in North Country have concluded in as little as two hours... more

Featured Listing:

Beautiful three bedroom, 2 ½ bath townhome with 2 ½ car garage, walk-in closet in master bedroom, fireplace, air conditioning, three balconies, patio and pool. Overlooks San Luis Rey Training Center and close to several golf courses. Just 15 minutes from the beach!!

Now accepting offers between $360,000 and $380,000.
Learn more

5. CREATING NEWSLETTER CONTENT

Perhaps one of the biggest concerns you have is the task of creating interesting content for your e-mail newsletter. "I'm not a writer," you say. Well, this chapter will dispel that concern. When you complete this chapter, you will be confident of your ability to prepare exciting newsletters that contain valuable information.

Creating informative articles is not as difficult as you imagine. There are a host of sources from which you can extract – or just plain copy – stories that will interest your readers. And remember, you only have to come up with two or three articles every month. Moreover, this undertaking can be a joint project by all the people in your office who are doing newsletters. After all, you're not (or shouldn't be) sending the same newsletter to the same clients and prospects. Approaching this as a group effort makes content preparation a painless exercise.

In this chapter, you will learn where to get materials for your articles, what types of articles you should create or seek, and how to position those in your newsletter to guarantee capturing the attention of your readers. The end result will be further enhancement of your image as a competent authority on the subject of real estate, someone with whom prospective customers feel comfortable in trusting with important financial transactions.

What Topics Should I Cover in my E-mail Newsletter?

An important first step is to determine what is of interest to your prospective readers. Put yourself in their shoes. Here are some questions to ask yourself:

- What real-estate related topics are of interest to my target market? Is it mortgage rates? Property values? Equity loans? Closing costs? The escrow process? How appraisals determine market value? A piece of legislation that could affect property taxes?

- Why types of questions have you and your associates been asked lately? These may indicate an interest in understanding the escrow or loan process, for example, or how a local school bond might affect future property values. Is a major road improvement scheduled to begin soon, and what impact could that have on local residents? Are new zoning laws being considered? Is a new shopping center or theme park planned for the area? Maybe it's what to do in the event of an earthquake.

- Is there a real estate issue that is costing your clients money? Do you have a solution or suggestion on how to handle this problem? Maybe it's termite season. Is there a new regional development on the horizon, such as cable Internet? Perhaps your readers would be interested in knowing how to do simple home repairs or where to get assistance.

- Do you have any new business programs or services to introduce to clients? Or, use your newsletter to explain the direct benefits of an existing program.

- Are there any promotional offers (e.g., no closing costs for the next 30 days!) that you wish to communicate to your market?

The point is, there are a multitude of relevant subjects about which plenty of information is available. All you have to do is scratch your head and think a little. Look in the local newspaper to get ideas or brainstorm with other people in your office. Surf real estate sites on the Web. Ask your clients what they would like to see in a newsletter. Use your imagination and the ideas will come quickly.

It is important to keep the topics related to real estate. One of the purposes in generating a newsletter is to reinforce your image to clients as an expert in the real estate market. So, don't pack your newsletter with recipes, local gossip, national news, a review of the school play or photos from your family vacation. Your readers can get that information elsewhere. Give them interesting, valuable information related to real estate and real estate only!

Pitching Your Articles

When your e-mail is opened, you have a just a few seconds to capture the reader's interest. Most recipients will immediately scan the headlines for the stories you've included to see if there is anything worthwhile for them. If not, you are likely to lose them and they will delete the e-mail.

The more time readers spend perusing your e-mail, the more likely they are to become familiar with your face and name. When this happens, your readership is apt to try some of the other links in the newsletter, such as the one leading to all your listings, or jumping to a Webpage containing your biography, or learning more about the programs your brokerage offers when selling a home. In short, the articles in your newsletter are the "honey" along the path to an action you would like readers to ultimately take.

To capture reader attention, not only must the subject matter be relevant, but you also need strong headlines. You want to entice recipients into opening articles, thus investing more time digesting your newsletter and linked materials. Reprint relevant articles, but make dull headlines more exciting within your newsletter. Digest an article in a newspaper, magazine or on the Web and create your own article by extracting the significance for the real estate market. Create you own articles. Whatever you do, make sure the newsletter headline for an article is sufficiently provocative to capture interest among your intended audience.

Spice up your headlines up a little. Let's look at some examples:

Original Article Headline	Suggested Newsletter Headline
"Fed Fails to Raise Interest Rates"	"Lending Rates Remain Low"
"Housing Starts Fail to Satisfy Demand"	"It's a Seller's Market!"
"New Highway Expected to Increase Local Traffic"	"Local Home Values Affected by Proposed Highway"
"City Council Passes Aid Program for First-Time Buyers"	"Exciting Program for First-Time Buyers!"
"Student Sign-Ups at Midtown College Drop Off"	"Local Rental Market Impacted by Student Decline"
"Local School Bond Passes"	"Your Real Estate Taxes May Increase"
"It's Termite Season Again"	"Protect Your Home Against Termites!"
"Local Home Prices Increase"	"Home Values Keep Going Up!"

Ideally, your newsletter should only present a lead-in (i.e., the first few sentences or first paragraph) of an article – or a summary of the main point(s) – before the reader must link to a Web page to view the complete article. This accomplishes two things: 1) It allows you to include more material in your newsletter, and 2) it gets prospects to your Website where you can offer links to additional pages you wish them to visit, such as your other listings, an offer for a free value assessment, a menu of loan programs, etc.

If you are preparing a self-contained, text-oriented newsletter, only present abbreviated stories. Lengthy stories are not suitable for this format. Readers are likely to get bored scrolling a long textual e-mail compared to navigating a graphical Webpage.

Sources for Article Content

Once you get into it, you will be surprised how easy it is to generate or find stories to place in your newsletter. In fact, there are many Web sources that allow you to freely use their articles for this purpose!

Let's explore the approaches you can follow to create content for your newsletter:

Method	Description
Create the article yourself	If you have the inclination and writing skills, this is excellent opportunity for you to create articles based on your own research. Moreover, you can use your article for multiple purposes, such as publishing on your Website or placement in a national online or printed publication.

Method	Description
Digest articles and create a synopsis	Similar to above, you can find several articles on a subject and write your own interpretation from a real estate perspective. Create new charts. Interview someone local for their reaction to the subject. To avoid being accused of plagiarism or violation of copyright laws, always include references for quotes or figures.
Simply reprint or summarize an existing article*	If the subject is right on target, take an article from your local newspaper or a press release and simply include it in your newsletter. Always indicate the title, author, media and date as given in the source publication. Do not copy articles from hard-copy or online magazines or other newsletters without first obtaining permission to do so.
Ask your business partners	Perhaps your business partners – lenders, escrow and title companies, appraisal firms – have relevant articles or information they are willing to share with you or allow you to publish.
Use articles from online real estate publications and Websites that authorize replication	Many real estate oriented Websites and online publications are willing to let you use their articles in your newsletter. They encourage this, as it gives them or the author free publicity.

*When reprinting an article in your newsletter, the best choice is to have the entire article reproduced on your Website to avoid losing the reader to other interests or even potential competitors that may be located on the article's resident Website. If you don't have a Website, you can either summarize the article in your newsletter or simply link to the article at its original Internet location.

On the next page are some sources where you can find relevant information for use in your newsletter:

Where to Find Free Articles

Some Websites allow you to reprint their articles in your own newsletter or to link to an article on the Website. In the case of links, the Websites below are not offering real estate services that would compete with your own business. Pay careful attention, however, to conditions and restrictions pertaining to article replications.

Table 1. Free Newsletter Content Sources

Website	Description
Total Real Estate Solutions http://www.totalrealestatesolutions.com	This Website is a real bonanza of information for real estate professionals. Contains many articles that may be reprinted in your newsletter (see "Real Estate Articles and Advice"). Articles which display the reprint permission icon may be reprinted provided that the original author profile information (including all links) is included with the article. You many not modify the article content or author profile information. Articles that do not contain the reprint icon may not be copied or distributed without obtaining permission from the original author. Please include the following courtesy notice on your reprint: Article reprinted courtesy of **Total Real Estate Solutions** http://www.totalrealestatesolutions.com
EzineArticles.com http://ezinearticles.com/	Offering free content for newsletters or Websites, these articles are produced by Realtors or lenders and cover such topics as "The Five Biggest Selling Mistakes."
Wealth Here http://www.wealthhere.com/free/	Offers free reprint of articles long as you leave the links and give author full credit in all of them OR you can also link directly to any of the reports on author's server.
The Real Estate Journal (WSJ) http://www.realestatejournal.com/	Produced by the Wall Street Journal, this offers a complete online guide to buying, selling and maintaining a home. Sign up for *their* e-mail newsletter to have potential articles delivered directly to your PC. Realtors may include a link to a RealEstateJournal.com article in their email newsletters at no charge. The link must go directly to the article on www.realestatejournal.com, without framing. Reprinting an article [i.e., placing the actual article in your newsletter] requires payment of a licensing fee.
Realty Times http://realtytimes.com/	Anyone can subscribe to Realty Times news and link to Realty Times news articles free of charge. These links can be placed on Websites and forwarded in e-mails. However, they do not allow their articles to be repackaged into newsletters, Websites, ads or any other personal or commercial marketing vehicle. The exception to this policy is for any Realtor or mortgage broker who is a paying subscriber to any Realty Times' marketing tools. Those subscribers may reprint Realty Times' stories as long as they give full attribution to Realty Times, the author, date of publication, and include the Realty Times URL - www.realtytimes.com. These articles may not be edited or altered in any way.

Website	Description
The REALTOR Magazine Online http://www.realtor.org/rmomag.NSF	According to the Realtor Website, you may copy and reprint an article IF the content you want to reprint is copyrighted by REALTOR® Magazine. To determine this, look at the source line at the bottom of the article. If the source line attribution is to NAR, REALTOR® Magazine, or REALTOR® Magazine Online, you have the right to reprint that article provided you use the reprint language below and follow the guidelines set forth here. If the source line does not attribute NAR, REALTOR® Magazine, or REALTOR® Magazine Online, that means REALTOR® Magazine does not hold the copyright and can't grant reprint rights. If you want to reprint an article that appeared in the site's news e-mail that is not attributed to NAR, REALTOR® Magazine, or REALTOR® Magazine Online, you must contact REALTOR® Magazine's news feed provider Information Inc. who holds the copyright for those articles. All articles copyrighted by Information Inc. that run in its daily or weekly news e-mail include a source line at the end of the story giving credit to the original source publication which include newspapers and wire services across the country. Information Inc. can be reached at 301/215-4688 or at http://www.infoinc.com/nar. Provide the date of the article and the name of the original publications indicated in the source line. **Second**, if the article's source line is attributed to NAR, REALTOR® Magazine, or REALTOR® Magazine Online, or if there is no source line included, the content is copyrighted by REALTOR® Magazine, and you may reprint the content, providing you credit the author, indicate the date of publication, include the appropriate reprint permission language and agree that content reproduced from REALTOR® Magazine will be reproduced in its entirety and will not be edited. **Your reprint permission language should appear as follows:** "Reprinted from REALTOR® Magazine with permission of the NATIONAL ASSOCIATION OF REALTORS®. Copyright 2004. All rights reserved." (**Note**: If the content appeared in REALTOR® Magazine in a year other than 2003, that year should be substituted in the permission language.)

Website	Description
The Phantom Writers http://thephantomwriters.com/free_content/d/w/real_estate_gurus.shtml	Free real estate article for potential investors.
All Free Spot http://www.allfreespot.com/art/contractking.html	They will e-mail you this article ("The Contract is King") in a format suitable for reprint in your newsletter.

Subscription Sources for Real Estate Articles

Some Websites require a subscription service to reprint (or link to) their articles in your own newsletters:

Table 2. Subscription Sources for Content

Website	Description
Copyright Clearance Center http://www.copyright.com/	The Digital Permissions Service connects you quickly to reuse rights from multiple publishers all in one place. The only charges you will be responsible for are the royalty fees set by the rights holder and a Copyright Clearance Center processing fee of $3.00 per granted request.
Inman News http://www.inman.com/	Daily real estate news and weekly newsletter. Offers 30,000 stories for your use in print publications and marketing materials for $149.95 annually.
SmartMoney Reprints http://www.smartmoney.com/reprints/	One-Year Web Posting Rights allow you to add SmartMoney's award-winning edit to your company's web offering. ePrint Rights allow you to email your clients and prospects a Custom SmartMoney Article Reprint as a PDF attachment. Contact Reprints Manager at (212) 373-9067 or email: reprints@smartmoney.com
Scoop ReprintSource http://www.scoopreprintsource.com/home/main.htm	Scoop ReprintSource offers a full line of reprint services, including the added benefit of "exclusive" relationships with numerous publications around the world. Must request quote for to place reprints in your newsletter.

Where to Find Real Estate Articles for Ideas or Quotes

Other Websites offer free articles that can be generally downloaded, BUT not included in your newsletter UNLESS you can obtain specific permission. However, this is a good way to get ideas for preparing your own articles and gathering accredited quotes for inclusion in those articles.

Table 3. Where to Find Articles

Website	Description
National Association of Realtors - Research Center http://www.realtor.org/rodesign.nsf/pages/researchctr?OpenDocument	Contains research on market trends, outlooks, data on home sales and press releases (which you can use in your newsletter).
RealEstateArticle.com http://www.realestatearticle.com/	The Website is a portal to a multitude of articles. Contact the source of each article for reprint rights.
RealEstateLink.Net http://www.realestatelink.net/	A resource Website for real estate investors. Contains many articles on subjects related to investing. Contact the source of each article for reprint rights.
Real Estate and Mortgage Resources www.real-estate.com	A resource Website with some article Web pages. Contact the Website for reprint rights.
American Real Estate Society (ARES) http://www.aresnet.org/	ARES, founded in 1985, serves the educational, informational, and research needs of leaders in the real estate industry and real estate professors at colleges and universities.
BusinessWeek Online http://www.businessweek.com/index.html	Good, national interest articles. To obtain reprint permission contact: The Copyright Clearance Center 222 Rosewood Drive Danvers, MA 01923. Tel: (978) 750-8400 Fax: (978) 750-4470
Appraisal Today http://www.appraisaltoday.com/	Articles related to appraisal industry.
Fannie Mae http://www.fanniemae.com/index.jhtml	Look under the section "For Home Buyers and Homeowners" where a wealth of information and tools are available. Contact Fannie Mae for reprint rights.

Website	Description
U.S. Department of Housing and Urban Development (HUD) http://www.hud.gov/news/index.cfm	Newsroom page has articles and press releases you can use in your newsletter. Be sure to check with HUD if copyrighted articles are used.
Freddie Mac http://www.freddiemac.com/	Contains an abundance of news releases, some of which may be appropriate to reprint for your market. If you are going to link to an external Website, this is a good one to use.
The Real Estate Library http://www.relibrary.com/	A bonanza of real estate information and gateways to useful information! Check out the "Real Estate News" section for content sources.
Newsletter Access http://www.newsletteraccess.com	Contains links to free real estate newsletters. Check each individually for reprint requirements. Also good place to get ideas about design layout for your newsletter.
Homeowner.com www.homeowner.com	Contains basic home buyer and owner information.
Real Estate Investing http://realestateinvesting.com/	Contains information and articles on real estate investing.
Yahoo Real Estate http://realestate.yahoo.com/	Contains a wealth of articles compiled from other sources. Contact the source of an article to ascertain reprint rights.
CRE Online.com http://www.real-estate-online.com/	Contains a large quantity of investing articles written by successful real estate investors. You must contact CRE for reprint rights.
MagPortal.com http://www.magportal.com/c/bus/ind/realty/	Contains a large quantity of investing articles written by successful real estate investors. You must contact CRE for reprint rights.
HomeFair.com www.homefair.com	Resource Website for buyers and sellers. You must contact HomeFair or its affiliates for reprint rights.
RisMedia.com http://www.rismedia.com	Contains press releases, stories and articles about latest real estate news. Offers FREE news feed and daily e-mails of latest news.
NewsCuts http://www.newscuts.com/Real.Estate.shtml	Offers real estate news and press releases from a variety of sources.

Website	Description
Pages http://www.pagesmag.com/3re-free.html	Subscription services that offers real estate related articles and artwork for newsletter insertion.

Directories for News Sources

If you had time to really dig into the Internet, you would discover that a plethora of real estate news and articles is available to help you develop content for your newsletter. Directories are Websites that contain links to other Websites where you can find press releases, articles and research information for preparing your newsletter content. Some directories you should investigate are:

Table 4. Directories for News Sources

Directory	Description
Like's E-News http://www.lukes.com/enews/	A News Portal for real estate savvy consumers and professionals, this Website contains links to a variety of online real estate publications.
1800miti.com http://www.1800miti.com/page76b-real.html	A News Portal for real estate trade journals and online news.
NAR Appraisal Section http://www.onerealtorplace.com	Portal for a variety of information and links concerning the appraisal profession.
Mortgage News Top Headlines http://www.mortgageleadguide.com	Portal that contains worldwide and domestic news on mortgage and real estate industry. Provides links to a variety of news feed sources.
Mortgage and Real Estate RSS News Feed Directory http://www.mortgageleadguide.com/Mortgage_Real_Estate_RSS_Directory.asp	Contains information and links to help you add a news feed to your Website.

6. BUILDING YOUR E-MAIL ADDRESS LIST

Before learning how to create e-mail newsletters on your personal computer, let's explore a critical step in conducting of e-mail marketing campaigns – how to create and manage an e-mail address lists.

Obviously, having an excellent newsletter does you no good unless your partners, customers and prospects have agreed to receive it. Recalling our discussion about "spamming" in Chapter 2, this means that they have "opted-in" or given their explicit consent to receive your newsletter. So, your first task is to acquire permission from intended recipients so you can send them your newsletter.

At first glance, this may seem to be a stumbling block to using e-mail newsletters for marketing purposes. Indeed, it takes some effort to initially compile a list of willing subscribers to your newsletter. But once this effort is completed, registration for your newsletter will gather its own momentum. In this chapter, you will learn a variety of tactics whose cumulative effect is to continually grow the subscription base for your newsletter. In fact, you can begin your solicitations while you are developing your newsletter.

Compiling a subscriber list is not as daunting a task as you may fear. You must first let everyone know that you have an e-mail newsletter and then solicit their permission to send it to them on a periodic basis, explaining that they can opt-out at any time. The secret is to employ multiple solicitation tactics in parallel to quickly build your initial list of opt-in subscribers. Once you have "primed the pump" with a core list of 25 or so subscribers, you will discover that sign-ups begin to happen on their own as your newsletter gets forwarded or referred to others. Continual promotion of your free newsletter to partners, customers and prospects is the will accelerate this trend.

What Information Do I Need?

When collecting a subscriber list, you want to make signing up fast and easy. Try to compile the following information:

Item	Why
Mandatory: First and Last Name	Allows you to personalize an introduction to your newsletter: "Dear Mr. Smith" or "Dear Tom:" "This is the first publication of an informative newsletter........"
Mandatory: E-Mail Address	You need this, obviously, to distribute your newsletter. Note that some people have more than one address, so ask which one is the best for this purpose. Ideally, you want to send it to their personal e-mail address that is read at home.

Item	Why
Optional: What e-mail application do they use?	You need to determine if they can receive graphical information (Word rich text format or HTML) or if a text-oriented e-mail is necessary. Most people are now capable of receiving e-mails with graphical content, but it pays to be sure. Also, if some people call or e-mail you to say that they are having problems with the format of your newsletter, you may be able to isolate it to a certain e-mail application (e.g., AOL) and take corrective steps.
Optional: Additional Contact Information	If feasible, always use communications with your clients as an opportunity to complete any missing information in their contact records.

How Should I Store This Information?

Unless you have list management software, initially store the collected information in your Microsoft Outlook Contacts, Access or other contact-management database (e.g., ACT or Goldmine). If you use Outlook, you may want to create a new Contact Category labeled "Newsletter" so that later you can easily identify which contacts have agreed to subscribe to your newsletter. An Outlook Contact record can belong to more than one Category. To duplicate an existing Contact record in your new Newsletter Category, just place a "," after the existing Category name in the existing Contact record and type in "Newsletter."

Alternatively, you can create a list in Excel that can later be imported into Outlook (the procedure is explained later in this chapter). If you do this, format your Excel worksheet with first row being a title line similar to the below example:

Last	First	E-Mail	Software (Optional)
Smith	John	jsmith@aol.com	AOL
Doe	Jane	jdoe@cox.net	Outlook
Adams	Brian	badames@earthlink.net	Netscape
Parsons	Jim	jbparsons@xyzcompany.com	Outlook

How Do I Develop A Subscription List?

A variety of tactics can be employed to build your subscription base. In all cases, the targets are your partners, customers and prospects. Use all or just some of the methods below as best suits your needs and resources. The more methods you use, the better the results you will see.

Regardless of the tactics employed, explain how your free newsletter will benefit the prospective subscriber (e.g., keeping them abreast of local real estate sales and trends, offering current mortgage rates and refinance news, or possibly alerting them to any events that could impact local values). Point out the unobtrusive frequency of the newsletter and emphasize that recipients have the option to unsubscribe at any time. Solicit your readers' input on what topics they would like to see addressed in the newsletter. Also emphasize that you respect their privacy and their e-mail addresses will not be given to anyone else.

Assuming you have an existing contact database, even it's only a Rolodex, this is the place to start. Here's how:

Phone Them!

Not only is this a good way to touch bases with everyone in contact database, it also gives you an opportunity to personally present your newsletter to prospective subscribers. Always ask if they know of anyone else who might be interested in the newsletter!

E-Mail Them

If you already have some e-mail addresses in your contact database, this is a productive means to get permission to send your newsletter to them. Prepare a standard text-based body for the e-mail, save it in Outlook Output (to use as a template) and then send it individually to each potential subscriber. Personalize the introduction of each e-mail to increase your success rate. Again, ask for referrals.

Explain how to sign-up by simply Replying to your e-mail with word "Subscribe" in the Subject line. Alternatively, include an embedded link in your e-mail "Click Here to Subscribe" that generates a Reply e-mail or else takes the reader to a Web-based registration form.

Deliver Flyers

Deliver flyers to your farm or territory (or hire someone to do it) promoting the benefits of subscribing to your newsletter. Include a sample screen shot of your newsletter within the flyer content. Explain how to sign-up for the newsletter by phoning you or simply sending you an e-mail with the words "Subscribe" in the Subject line. Remember to ask for their first and last name.

This approach works best when combined with a promotional offer, for example:

- "Sign-up includes registration for drawing of free 25" color TV" [or PDA, weekend getaway for two, DVD, etc.]

- "Free Lotto ticket to all that sign up"

- "Free matinee tickets to all those who register by Thursday" ["Free pass to...," etc.]

- "Sign up to receive a free assessment of your home's market value"

- "Subscribers pay zero closing costs" [for refinances]

Mail Postcards

Develop an attractive direct-mail piece promoting the benefits of subscribing to your newsletter. If possible, include a sample screen shot of your newsletter within the postcard content. Explain how to sign-up for the newsletter by phoning you or simply sending you an e-mail with the words "Subscribe" in the Subject line. Remember to ask for their first and last name. Again, this approach achieves a higher response rate when it includes a promotional offer.

Post Your Flyer or Direct-Mail Piece in Public Places

Post your solicitation material in public libraries, supermarkets or any other bulletin board when permissible.

Add a Tag Line to Your Business Card

It is assumed that your e-mail address is already on your business card. That said, verbally promote your newsletter every time you hand out a business card and include printed instructions for subscribing (on front or back of the card). Suggestions for wording are:

- "E-mail me for free, informative newsletter." [If you do not have a Website]

- "Subscribe to free monthly newsletter at www.abcrealty.com" when there is a sign-up option on your Website.

Create a Signature File for Your E-Mails

Create a personalized signature block for your outgoing e-mails which contains a tag line promoting your newsletter. Provides a means – or explain how – to subscribe. Consider these examples:

> *"Click Here to subscribe to a free, informative monthly newsletter."* [If you have a Website with subscriber registration form]

> *"Reply to this e-mail with "Subscribe" in the Subject Line to receive a free, informative newsletter."*

Add a Tag Line to Your Presentations

If you give presentations using overhead transparencies, slides or Microsoft PowerPoint, be sure to add a tag line to tile and closing slides to promote your newsletter.

Use Microsoft Outlook Contacts to Create a Distribution List

If you collected your opt-in data in Excel, export those names to Outlook. To see the procedure for accomplishing this, launch Excel then open its Help feature:

1. Using the *Help Answer Wizard*, type "Export Excel names to Outlook" in the *Search Box*
2. Select "*Share contact data between Excel and Outlook*" among the responses
3. Choose "*Export Microsoft Excel Names and Addresses to Outlook*" to access step-by-step instructions to complete the operation.

Once your opt-in names and e-mail addresses are loaded into Microsoft Outlook, the next step is to create a Distribution List called "Newsletter." If you have established a Contact Category named "Newsletter," locating the opt-in subscribers is as easy as opening this Category in your Outlook Contacts database.

A Distribution List is a collection of e-mail addresses under one Contact record. It allows you to send an Outlook e-mail to a group of people with a single click of the Send button. A message sent to a Distribution List is received by all those who are included in the List. To learn how to set up a "Newsletter" Distribution List, open Word Help and:

1. Type "Distribution List" in the *Search box*
2. Select "*Create a distribution list*"
3. Follow the instructions given there to either create a Distribution List from your Address Book or else to copy names from an e-mail.
4. Note that you must name and *Save* a Distribution List before you can use it!

Although an Outlook Distribution List allows you to send your e-mail newsletter to a group of recipients all at once, the downside is that each recipient sees not only their own name but also the names of all other recipients on the **To** line of the message (instead of seeing the name of the Distribution List). Thus, even though this is efficient, using an Outlook Distribution List is impersonal. Moreover, it may your market relationship because it does not protect individual e-mail addresses.

A workaround solution to avoid having a long list of e-mail addresses appearing in the **To** line of your e-mail is to create a dummy Distribution List name, such as "Newsletter Distribution" which contains only your e-mail address. Then use the blind-copy feature of Outlook ("**Bcc**") to send out your newsletter to the real distribution list. **Bcc** appears as an option in Outlook when you click on the **To** line in the process of creating a new e-mail message. Just place your real newsletter Distribution List name in the **Bcc** box. The recipient's name is not visible to other subscribers, and the recipient will only see your name in the **From** line.

The downside to this approach is that many desktop spam filters (discussed in the next chapter) will halt or pigeon-hole an e-mail with a large **Bcc** list. So, you may have to ask your subscribers to add your e-mails to their "cleared list" in Outlook. To do this, they must go to *Tools/Rules Wizard*/click *Exception List*/click *Add* and request them to enter your e-mail address. Messages sent from your e-mail address will thereafter appear in their Inbox as usual, even if your e-mail address is part of a domain (i.e., Website) listed in their Junk Senders list. Any rules applied to that domain will not be applied to you.

If you want to know when each of your clients opens your e-mail newsletter, request a read receipt. In the Outlook e-mail containing the newsletter in its body, go to *View/Options* and click the box entitled "*Request a read receipt for this message*." However, this procedure may be annoying to some people, so it is not recommended.

Thus, using an Outlook Distribution List for e-mailings is feasible but cumbersome and best limited to a small number of subscribers (say, 50 or less). In Chapter 8, you will learn a better way to manage e-mail lists that circumvents these shortcomings.

List Management

Regardless of the tools used to create and store your list of newsletter subscribers, careful attention is necessary to keep it current. Several events can occur that require modification of your subscriber list:

- The e-mail "bounces," meaning that the e-mail address could not be found. You will get an e-mail error message stating that the e-mail could not be delivered to a specific name on your Distribution List. This usually implies that the intended recipient has implemented a new e-mail address or discontinued his Internet service altogether. <u>Immediately remove the "bounced" e-mail address from your Distribution List and (if still present) delete the newsletter e-mail from your Outlook Output folder</u>. Otherwise, Outlook may continue to attempt deliveries to every name in your List, sending your newsletter to all valid e-mail addresses over and over again. This will not endear you to your subscribers. Phone or write the "bounced" client to update his e-mail address. Commercial software exists to automatically handle "bounced" e-mails and avoid the problems these can create.

- New subscribers must be added. Open the Distribution List, and then click "*Update Now*" to add a new subscriber. Ideally, you also should send a confirmation notice to a new subscriber, thanking them and letting them know that they will receive the next edition of your newsletter. You can create a standard text message in Word for this purpose and then *Copy/Paste* it into an addressed e-mail to the new subscriber to *Send*.

- People who "unsubscribe" must be deleted from your Distribution List. Follow the above instructions (Update Now) to delete an e-mail from your Distribution List. Again, a confirmation e-mail back to the "unsubscriber" is recommended.

You may wish to create different Distribution Lists for different purposes. Perhaps you have a graphical newsletter for one group and a text-oriented newsletter for another set of clients. Maybe you have different newsletters for different neighborhoods or classes of clients. As you gain experience with e-mail newsletters, you will probably explore segmenting your market for maximum effectiveness of the message being delivered.

List management is a never-ending task, one that must be accomplished manually when using Microsoft Outlook Distribution Lists. There are also limitations inherent in Outlook which, when combined with restrictions implemented by your company's Microsoft Exchange Server or your Internet Service Provider (ISP), can create problems. Reference Microsoft Outlook Help under "Troubleshooting distribution lists" if you experience problems – there may be a workaround solution. <u>Failure to keep on top of list management can have dire consequences</u>, including alienating your clients, which defeats the purpose of the newsletter altogether.

Fortunately, commercial software and free desktop solutions exist which circumvent the list management shortcomings of Microsoft Outlook. These are discussed in later Chapters.

7. USE YOUR PC TO CREATE AND DISTRIBUTE ATTRACTIVE NEWSLETTERS

By now, you have a basic understanding of e-mail newsletters, you know how to acquire and present content for your articles, and how to build and manage your e-mail list using Microsoft Outlook. Let's now turn our attention to the creation of a professional-looking newsletter using your personal computer.

A recent survey indicated that about 90 percent of e-mail recipients prefer to receive a graphical newsletter and up to 99 percent are *capable* of receiving these types of e-mail newsletters. So, from this point forward, the focus will be on developing and managing graphically-oriented newsletters in Microsoft Word.

Preparing and delivering a monthly or quarterly graphical newsletter on your own is not only feasible, but also a low-cost undertaking. Although there are some limitations to this approach, they can be circumvented by spending just a little money to acquire commercial software to enhance your productivity (see Chapter 7). For now though, we will begin by explaining the steps in developing a newsletter format, then inserting links and content.

The reader is referred to an online Microsoft resource, http://office.microsoft.com/, for step by step guidance in creating an online newsletter using Word. If you have Office 2002 or later, Microsoft even includes a template that can be customized for your purpose:

1. Using your Internet browser, go to http://office.microsoft.com/templates/
2. Type in "real estate e-mail newsletter" in the *Search box* and click "Go"
3. Save the Word Template on your local drive
4. Customize the template to suit your needs

Like any Word-based template, you can personalize it any way you wish. For example:

*   Change the table column or row widths and lengths
*   Change the fonts and colors
*   Change the table shading
*   Change the links or insert new ones
*   Replace the graphics with your own selection, or insert photos.

A template is just a starting point. Everything is customizable in a template to suit your needs.

This Chapter shows you how to easily create your own newsletter templates from scratch. Then we will go beyond that, learning how to save your finished Word-based newsletter in a filtered Hyper-Text Markup

Language (HTML) format for best e-mail performance and formatting results. HTML is the language that Web pages are written in. Finally, you will learn where to get free newsletter templates off the Web!

Creating Your Newsletter

Unless you have an HTML editor, newsletter design on your desktop PC is best accomplished using Microsoft Word. Since the final format of the newsletter will be transformed to HTML, select Web layout in Word for your View (View/Web Layout).

When using Word, the underlying structure of the newsletter is a "table" with one, two or three columns. A "cell" is a box formed within the table by the intersection of a row and column. Information is entered in the cells of a table. For example, the below table contains two columns, two rows and four cells:

	Column 1	Column 2
Row 1	Cell 1	Cell 2
Row 2	Cell 3	Cell 4

If you need assistance in creating a table, open Word Help and type "create table" in the Search box, then select "Create Table" from the options to get specific instructions.

Important operations you need to understand to work with tables to create your newsletter are:

Operation	Description
"Grabbing" and *"Dragging"* borders to resize a table, column or row	To "grab" a border, place the cursor on the border until the cursor changes to two parallel lines. Click and hold the left mouse button to "drag" the border to its desired location. The vertical length of a row can also be increased or decreased by simply hitting the Return or Backspace (or Delete) keys respectively. Experiment with this to get the idea.
Splitting cells 1. Select (i.e., highlight) cell to be split 2. Right-click mouse and choose *Split Cell* 3. Specify number of columns or rows to create	To "split" a cell into one or more columns or rows, place your cursor within the targeted cell and right-click your mouse to get a pop-up menu. Choose *Split Cells* to launch a dialogue box that let's you specify the number of columns or rows to be created within the selected cell.
Merging cells 4. Select (i.e., highlight) cells to be merged 5. Right-click mouse and choose *Merge Cells*	Highlight two or more cells to be merged into one cell. Right-click your mouse to get a pop-up menu. Choose *Merge Cells* to change the highlighted cells into a single cell.

Operation	Description
Changing the *Shading* for borders and cells 1. Click cursor on table or select a specific cell 2. Right click the mouse to get pop-up menu 3. Choose *Borders and Shading*	Using your mouse, *Select* the cell you wish to modify (or *Select* the entire table if that is your objective). *Right click* your mouse to get a pop-up menu and select "*Borders and Shading...*" This opens a dialogue box where you can change the color of specific table and cell borders (*Border* tab), or the background color for the table or a selected cell (*Shading* tab). To change the entire table color, your cursor can reside anywhere within the table. To modify the color of a specific cell, select the individual cell first.
Changing the font type, size and color within a cell 1. *Select* the text to be modified 2. Click on *Format/Font* on main Word menu.	Using your mouse, *highlight* the text or font to be modified and click on *Format* in the main Word menu. Choose *Font*, which launches a dialogue box allowing you to change the size, type and/or color of the selected font within the current cell only. This box also allows you to modify the character spacing and to insert special effects for the selected text.
Inserting graphics and photos with a cell 1. *Select* targeted cell 2. Click on *Insert/Picture, Insert/Diagram* or *Insert/Object*	Place your cursor in the targeted cell where the insertion is desired. Click on *Insert* in the main Word menu; choose *Picture, Diagram* or *Object* to launch dialogue boxes for completing the operations.
Resizing a photo or graphic 1. Select photo or graphic to be resized 2. Hold down Ctrl key and drag a corner towards center until desired sizing is achieved.	Click on the picture, diagram or object and simply "*grab*" a corner. While holding down the *Control* key (to maintain proportion), *drag* the mouse towards the center of the selected entity until the desired sizing is achieved.
Creating *Headings* Note: Only use this feature if you have an HTML editor or plan to deliver your newsletter in PDF format. Otherwise, the Word-based attributes will be lost when converted to HTML.	For ease of creating internal hyperlinks (see below), change your article headlines to a *Heading 1* style *highlighting* each in turn and selecting this choice on the roll-down menu in the main Word menu (next to the font type). This will allow you to later link an internal table of contents with the appropriate article headline.
Hyperlink internal text to an external Web page or other internal text 1. *Select* the text, photo or graphic to be linked 2. *Insert/Hyperlink*	Highlight the text, photo or graphic for which a link is to be created. Right-click the mouse and choose *Hyperlink* to launch a dialogue box. Choose either *Existing File or Web Page* (to link to an external Website) or *Place in This Document* (to link to a set of text within your newsletter. For the former, you must provide the URL of the Web page to which the reader's Web browser will go. For an internal link, the text to which you wish the reader to be transferred (i.e., the Header text for an article) must be a Heading type (1, 2, 3, etc.) which can be selected within the launched dialogue box. Once the link is established, clicking on the respective text, photo or graphic will take the reader to the linked destination.

Operation	Description
Adding or *Deleting* columns or rows. 1. *Select* a row or column to be deleted, or 2. Select the row or column which indicates a location within your table to add a row or column 3. *Table/Insert* or *Table/Delete* 4. Choose *Row* or *Column*	To correct mistakes or change existing layouts, you can add or delete a row or column by first *highlighting* it (i.e., *Select* the entire row or column), then using the main Word menu, choose *Table/Insert* or *Table/Delete* and specify the operation you wish to perform (choose *Row* or *Column*).

Once you have mastered these operations, you can create a variety of professional-looking newsletters that will "wow" your clients!

Typically, tables used to create newsletters have up to three columns and three-to-four rows. For ease of reader navigation and conformance with the expected location of links and information, three generic table layouts are recommended:

1. One column, one row:

All links, articles, graphics and photos are included in a single cell. User navigation is achieved by scrolling the newsletter up or down, or by clicking on a table of contents link to jump to a desired article.

2. Two columns, three-to-four rows:

Photos or logos	Headings/Title
Volume or Edition Number and Date	
Hyperlinked Table of Contents ("In This Issue") Links to: External Web pages Your Listings Promotional Offers Forward to a Friend Subscribe Etc. Contact Information	Lead-In Articles (Headlines and Summaries) Links to external Web pages for remainder of story, to learn more about a program or offer, etc.
Unsubscribe Information	

Notice the use of *merging* operations on the second and fourth rows. Also, the middle column border was *dragged* leftward to create the desired layout. Alternatively, it could have been *dragged* rightward to create a mirror copy of the above layout.

3. Three columns, three-to-four rows:

Photos or logos	Headings/Title	
Volume or Edition Number and Date		
Hyperlinked Table of Contents ("In This Issue") Links to: External Web pages Your Listings Promotional Offers Forward to a Friend Subscribe Etc. Contact Information	Lead-In Articles (Headlines and Summaries) Links to external Web pages for remainder of story, to learn more about a program or offer, etc.	External Links: Advertisements Product Photos Etc.
Unsubscribe Information		

Similar to the second example (above), except a third column has been added by splitting the middle-right cell into two columns, then dragging the column borders to achieve the desired re-alignment.

Design Tips

Before creating your newsletter in Word, here are some helpful tips that will result in appealing designs and circumvent problems with different browsers and Internet Service Providers (ISPs):

- Use a table-based structure to create you newsletter. Avoid use of esoteric Word features, as these may not translate well to non-Outlook e-mail applications or generic HTML layouts.

- Use complementary colors to fill your cell backgrounds (i.e., use colors that go well together). Look at the e-mail newsletters you now receive to get some ideas. A good approach is to use the same color in different intensities. Limit the number of colors in your e-mail to two or three. Exception, the background color for the bottom "Footer" line can be left as white or even be a different (but subtle) color entirely.

- Don't get wild - Limit your font types to no more than two. A suggestion is to use Times Roman or Courier for the Title and Arial or Courier for the body of the newsletter. Limit the number of photos and graphics to those necessary, as these add time to downloading e-mails (especially in a dial-up mode).

- Avoid the use of bullets (numbering is OK).

- Don't cram stuff together! Use spacing to open up the newsletter and make it more readable and aesthetically appealing.

- For those of you who are technically sophisticated, curtail your inclinations and keep it simple – avoid Java scripts, Active-X, etc., that may get killed by a spam blocker or other security barriers.

- Do use photos and graphics to liven up your newsletter. If you don't already have one, have a professional-looking photograph of yourself prepared in business attire. Photos should be in JPEG or GIF format to reduce their storage size (never use TIFF!!). Check the tag after the photo name to verify its format (e.g., realtor.jpg for a JPEG photo).

- If you have an HTML editor, do create an internal, hyperlinked table of contents so that readers can quickly determine what might be of interest to them and then jump to it.

- Ideally, present only a lead-in or summary of your articles, linking the reader to go to a Web page to digest the entire article. If you don't have a Website where your articles can be placed, then summarize the article. Remember, newsletters should be kept short and informative!

- Article headlines should be in bold font and at least one size larger than the underlying article text. In addition, using a different color for the headline is fine if it fits within the overall color scheme.

- Underline or use a consistent color for links (e.g., blue) – this helps readers to quickly identify or locate them.

- Get at least two people to proofread your newsletter, assess its design and test its links BEFORE sending it out.

Choose the Format for Your Newsletter

If you are using your desktop PC to create and send a newsletter, then you have two choices when it comes to actually distributing your e-mail (excluding text-based newsletters):

1. HTML (HyperText Markup Language) – This is the common format for newsletters that are distributed not only from a Website but also within the body of e-mails. HTML is low on size and accepted by most Internet e-mail applications today. To transform your newsletter from Word into HTML:

- Open your Word-based newsletter (*File/Open/your newsletter location*)

- Save it as a "*filtered* HTML" file under a different name in a (perhaps new) folder called "*My Newsletters*." The command for this is *File/Save As/Choose Folder/Type = Web Page, Filtered*. This preserves your master template or current newsletter in a modifiable Word format that allows future alterations (HTML documents cannot be modified without an HTML editor).

- Note that some unique Word attributes are lost when saving a document in a filtered HTML format. That's why it's best to avoid using bullets or internal hyperlinks when creating your newsletter in Word. It is also why you should use *Web View* when creating your newsletter to ensure that what you see is what you get.

2. Adobe PDF – An alternative to HTML, PDF creates a small-sized transformation of your e-mail into an unalterable form. PDF is commonplace, and PDF documents are sent as attachments to e-mails. PDF documents are easy to create, do not contain viruses and usually survive commercial spam filters.

   To transform a document to PDF, an Adobe write tool called "Distiller" is necessary. This tool can be purchased from Adobe or resellers for $150-$200. A less expensive alternative is offered by BCL Technologies (http://www.bcltechnologies.com/document/products/easypdf/easypdf.htm). Called "BCLeasyPDF," it sells for just $49! Another package, "pdf 995" is available for FREE (http://www.pdf995.com) if you are agreeable to advertising appearing in your Internet browser when pdf 995 is open. Otherwise, a "key" can be purchased for $9.95 to run it without advertising.

   Rather than purchase a desktop PDF converter, however, FREE online services are available to convert your newsletter to PDF format:

   - goBCL.com (http://www.gohtm.com/)

   - PDF Converter.com (http://www.pdfconverter.com/)

   The downside of using PDF, of course, is that you have to open an attachment to see it. This requires that the reader have the Adobe PDF Reader (free) installed on his/her desktop. With an HTML newsletter, your client gets the visual impact immediately upon opening the e-mail.

Copying your Word-based newsletters in Rich Text Format into the body of an e-mail is not appropriate for e-mail newsletters. It may look fine on *your* desktop, but it is likely that some recipients will receive format errors and strange characters in their text. Worse yet, embedded photos and clipart will be lost when the e-mail is forwarded to someone else.

A last statement about text-based newsletters: If you encounter any difficulties that cannot be solved, extract your text, delete the photos and clipart, and resort to a text-based e-mail newsletter until the graphics' issues are resolved.

Step-By-Step Example – Developing a Graphical Newsletter

Okay. It is time for you to create a sample newsletter using Microsoft Word. Fire up your PC, open Microsoft Word and follow the below process:

1. Create a structural layout using a *Table* consisting of two columns and four rows:

   a. Create a table (*Table/Insert/Table – Columns=2;Rows=4*):

   b. *Grab* the middle column border and drag it to the left:

   c. Merge the cells in Rows 2 and 4 (*Select* the cells one row at a time and *right-click/Merge*):

   d. Insert complementary background colors into your basic design structure (*Select* the cells (they turn dark when selected), *right-click/Borders and Shading/Shading/pick appropriate colors for each cell*):

e. Select entire top row and make the middle column border invisible (select row/right-click/Borders and Shading/Borders/choose "None" setting). Insert a photo or logo into the upper left cell (Insert/Picture). Resize and Center it, adding a name if appropriate:

Note that the photo can be selected and a hyperlink inserted so that if the reader clicks on it, they will launch their Internet browser and be transferred to your personal Website (if you have one).

f. Add the newsletter Title, using size 24 bold Times New Roman font in dark blue:

g. Add information to the second roll, such as a caption, newsletter volume number and/or date. Here, Arial size 10 bold font in white color is used:

h. Add sample articles to the right cell of row 3 as shown here. Use size 12 Arial Black font for headlines. Remember to change the headlines from "normal" to "Heading 1" if you want to an internal, hyperlinked table of contents (not recommended unless the newsletter is created with an HTML editor). Normal Arial size 10 font is used for the article text. Use left-justified text. Only article lead-ins are used in these examples. The reader must click on "more" (blue is used to indicate a link) to access a full article on your company or personal Website. If you do not have a linkable Website, then summarize the article here.

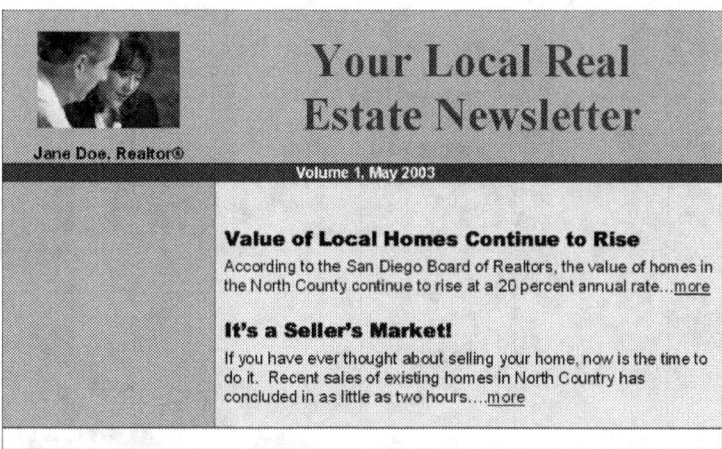

i. Add a "Featured Listing" following your articles. Including a photo makes it more attractive. Size the photo (by clicking on it and holding down the Ctrl key while dragging a corner to desired size) and text as necessary for formatting. Add text below the photo. Note that the vertical length of the cell expands as text is added. Insert a link to access full information about the listing on your company or personal Website (if you have one) in a section where all your listings exist for the reader's perusal.

j. If your newsletter is to be hosted on a Website or you intend to enhance it with an HTML editor, add an internal table of contents to the left cell of row 3 (which is hyperlinked to the relevant article for ease of navigation). In any case, add links in the left cell of row 3 to your Website (if you have one). For consistency purposes and reader recognition, underline text which is hyperlinked to internal or external destinations.

k. Finally, add legal information and unsubscribe instructions (centered) in the bottom row. The link here goes to a list management package running on your Website or that of a third-party service provider. If you do not have a Website or Web-based service, the appropriate instruction would be: "If you do not wish to receive future newsletters, please Reply to this e-mail and type "Remove" in the subject line."

To deter your work from being misappropriated by someone else, be sure to insert a copyright statement at the bottom. In the USA, almost everything created privately and originally after April 1, 1989 is copyrighted and protected whether it has a notice or not. However, having a copyright notice is still recommended, as it will give a potential rip-off artist pause. So, be sure to include a copyright statement at the bottom of your newsletter, such as "Copyright© 2004 ABC Realty – All Rights Reserved" or "Copyright© 2004 Jane Doe – All Rights Reserved."

To help you get ideas for your newsletter layout, take a look at the newsletters you yourself now receive. Go to a variety of Websites to review their newsletters. With these examples in mind, you should have no problem in developing an attractive design that suits your purpose.

Free Newsletter Templates

As you have seen, creating your own graphical newsletter template is not difficult. Modifying an existing newsletter template is even easier. Fortunately, there are FREE templates that can be downloaded from the Web to get you off to a fast start. Most of these are based on the HTML format, so you will need to download a free (what you see is what you get – WYSIWYG) HTML editor (discussed later) to modify them. You can change the structural layout, modify colors, change fonts and, of course, replace the content with your own.

Where can you find FREE templates? The first one to look at is the Microsoft Word template mentioned earlier in this chapter. Go to http://office.microsoft.com/templates and type "real estate" in the search box to download this template as a Word document. You can also download a wealth of FREE real estate business photos and clipart from this site.

Do a Google search for "free newsletter templates." A few of the many Websites that offer FREE templates to assist you in your newsletter development are:

- http://www.emaildesigntemplates.com/freetemplates.html offers three free HTML newsletter templates
- http://www.newz2me.com/ offers FREE text-based templates. The Website that also offers FREE Website templates and tutorials.
- http://homebiztools.com/newsletter-templates.htm provides a FREE newsletter template and advice on newsletter construction.
- http://www.myfreetemplates.com/category/56 provides some very nice FREE HTML-based newsletter templates that can be downloaded for your use. You will need an HTML editor, however, to modify these.
- http://www.free-newslettertemplates.com/ also offers FREE newsletter templates for both text- and HTML-based formats.
- http://www.sparklist.com/services/htmltemplates.html provides FREE HTML-based newsletter templates that can be downloaded for your use.
- http://www.alouwebdesign.ca/free/free-email-template/free-email-template-instructions.html offers FREE HTML newsletter templates.
- http://www.newsletterpromote.com/emailtemp/free.htm provides FREE HTML-based newsletter templates that can be downloaded for your use.
- http://www.mach5.com/products//templates/ offers three FREE e-mail newsletter templates.

Where Can I Find Additional Information About Preparing E-Mail Newsletters?

In addition to the Websites listed above, several exist on the Internet to broaden your background in e-mail newsletters. These sites offer technical Q&A pages plus helpful hints in designing and marketing your newsletter. Particularly good sites to visit are:

- Ezine University (http://ezineuniversity.com/). EzineUniversity exists to help you become a successful E-Zine (i.e., an e-mail newsletter or other online publication) Publisher. Several leading online experts share their expertise with you in this educational forum. The site even offers a FREE handbook and several online courses.

- E.Business Resource Center (http://www.zeromillion.com/ebiz/). A resource for all levels of businessmen, businesswomen, entrepreneurs, and marketers, this site offers several interesting articles on e-mail newsletter development.

- E-Mail Marketing Resources (http://www.benchmarkemail.com/emailresources.asp). This site provides a list (with links) of Websites that might prove useful to you.

- Courses and resources about desktop publishing can be found at "About" (http://desktoppub.about.com/cs/software/).

Save a Master Template

Before proceeding, run *Spell Check* and *Save* your newsletter as a Word document on your hard disk drive in a folder labeled "Newsletter Template." You now have a master template that you can be used for subsequent editions of your newsletter. From now on, all you have to do to create a new newsletter is to modify the content in column 2 (articles and Featured Listing). Every newsletter you send out will thus have a consistent "look and feel," making it easier for your clients to recognize and navigate its contents.

Getting Your Newsletter Ready for Distribution

Now that your graphical e-mail newsletter is prepared and formatted, ask yourself "In what format do I want to distribute this? If you choose a PDF format, then convert it using Adobe Distiller, BCLeasyPDF or pdf 995 on your desktop PC or by signing up for a free online service. If you elect to distribute it in HTML format embedded in the body of an e-mail, there are still a few tests and cautions to take before sending it.

Make Sure Your E-Mail Application is Formatted for "HTML"

In order to properly display an e-mail whose body contains HTML material, your e-mail application must be set to the proper format. Most e-mail applications, such as Outlook, are commonly set to this format, but it pays to be sure. Here's the procedure for Outlook:

- In Outlook, go to *Tools/Options/Mail Format*

- At the top of the dialogue box, make sure that "*Compose in this message format*" is set to "*HTML*" (instead of "*Plain Text*" or "*Rich Text*").

This setting allows you send and receive e-mail messages in HTML format.

Take It for a Test Drive

With your newsletter open in the Web Layout view format (View/Web Layout) within Word, perform Edit/Select All/Copy, then Insert/Paste into the body of a new blank e-mail. You should now see your HTML newsletter displayed in the body of the e-mail. Make sure everything is as it should be – are there any formatting errors? Are all photos, clipart, etc., displayed and in the correct location? If not, make sure your e-mail application is properly set for HTML messages.

In addition to having one or more people proofread your newsletter for spelling, grammar and comprehension errors, establish a network wherein you can have the newsletter "forwarded" several time, winding up back in your e-mail Inbox. Have your network of friends immediately notify you if they encounter any formatting errors, strange characters, or dropped photos/graphics along the way.

Note that embedded photos and graphics may not retain their formatting in recipient e-mail applications other than Microsoft Outlook. Netscape, AOL, Eudora, and Lotus Notes e-mail each has idiosyncrasies that can disrupt formatting. In most cases, such disruption will not be severe. Ideally, however, check your graphical e-mail out on PCs using non-Microsoft e-mail. In some cases (if distortions are significant), you may want to send a text-based e-mail newsletter to certain clients.

Virus Check

The last thing you need is a computer virus hitchhiking on your newsletter. If you have not done so already, acquire McAfee or Norton virus protection for your desktop PC and be sure to keep it up to date. Subscribing to an online version ensures that updates are automatically installed as they become available.

Spam Check

You don't want your newsletter to be blocked by a spam filter. If you already have a spam filter, one way to test this is to send your e-mail newsletter to yourself. If it gets blocked, find out what spam filter criteria is tripping it up and make changes accordingly. For those who don't have a filter installed, you can acquire a FREE filter off the Web:

- SPAMfighter is a FREE Microsoft Outlook plug-in (www.spamfighter.com)

- For others, check http://email.about.com/cs/winspamreviews/tp/free_spam.htm which provides a review of the top 10 FREE spam filters.

In some cases, your Internet Service Provider (ISP) may be blacklisted because of persistent complaints that it is allowing spammers to flood the Internet. If this occurs, contact your ISP. If the situation cannot be resolved, switch to a new ISP. Also, once you get going, avoid using a free e-mail service to distribute your newsletter - it is more likely to get blocked and, besides, looks unprofessional.

Distribute Your Newsletter

In Chapter 5, we discussed how to send your e-mail newsletter using a Distribution List created in Microsoft Outlook Contacts. As indicated there, a lot of housekeeping is involved in maintaining a mail list. New subscribers must be added and should be sent a confirmation notice. Those who unsubscribe must be deleted from your list. Of course, a strong drawback to using Microsoft Outlook for list management is that all of your e-mail addresses are exposed in the "To" line, which could alienate clients concerned about privacy. It also looks impersonal and seems unprofessional. Using Bcc to blind copy subscribers has drawbacks too – your newsletter may be blocked by a spam filter.

Automate Your List Management

The solution to this dilemma is "list management" software. Typical list management applications automate housekeeping tasks and help you to achieve more professionalism is presenting your newsletter to clients. The major functions performed by list management solutions are:

Function	Description
Sign up new subscribers	This software opens a "registration page" on a Website or your desktop PC where subscriber information, such as name and e-mail address, can be collected and stored in a database. A link to your "privacy policy" is usually included as well to calm any fears potential subscribers may have about you sharing or selling their e-mail address to bulk mail vendors. New subscribers should receive a confirmation e-mail with a greeting from you to ensure they are aware of their subscription.
Send a confirmation notice to new subscribers	An automated confirmation notice can be sent to new subscribers. This usually thanks the subscriber, explains if further action is required to confirm the subscription (e.g., click on this link…), tells them when they will receive their first issue and explains how to unsubscribe if they so wish.
Sends out your newsletter to all subscribers, but only shows an individual client's name and/or e-mail address in the "**To**" line	List management software and services allow fast distribution of your newsletter to *all* subscribers, while making it appear that an individual e-mail is being sent to *each* subscriber.

Function	Description
Supports personalization of your e-mails	Personalization of your e-mail creates rapport with the client and increases readership. Most list management programs include mail merge capabilities to personalize each email that you send. For example, this may allow: • Insertion of the client's first name in the **Subject** line along with your newsletter notice • Insertion of first and/or last name of the recipient into boiler-plate text in the e-mail body as a lead-in to your newsletter. • The ability to mail-merge data into specific areas of your lead-in text.
Handles bounced e-mail	If a subscriber discontinues his e-mail address (e.g., changed his ISP) or his mailbox is full, your e-mail newsletter will be undeliverable. A "bounced" e-mail notification will be sent to you and the address deleted or frozen awaiting your follow-up action.
Handles "Unsubscribe" requests	Automates the process of removing the e-mail addresses of those who follow your procedures for unsubscribing. May also send an automatic "confirmation" notice.
Allows you to segment your e-mail list	If you have more than one newsletter or different categories of clients, a typical list management package will support different e-mail lists for different purposes.
Automatically sends either an HTML- or text-based newsletter depending upon the addressee's e-mail settings	Uses a technique known as "multi-part MIME" to send out messages. When an HTML email is sent in multi-part MIME, clients who do not have the ability to view graphical newsletters will receive their newsletter in a text format.
Schedules personalized messages to your subscribers	If you know, for example, when a client's birthday is, a list management package could be configured to automatically send a birthday greeting!

Many list management applications also contain templates and HTML editors to assist you in creating newsletters, as well as pre-formatted registration pages and workflow processes. Some will provide standard subscribe/unsubscribe HTML-based boilerplate to place at the bottom of your newsletter.

Free List Management Services

If you initially have less than 50 clients or so who subscribe to your e-mail newsletter, you may want to consider a free service that handles list management over the Internet. While several online services offer this function for free, the downside is that your subscribers must go to a Website that includes advertising to subscribe or modify their account data. Also, some services send out advertisements or a tag-line with the e-mail containing your newsletter. But this is a small price to pay when you are first starting out, especially for the capabilities gained with professional list management. Yahoo! Groups (http://groups.yahoo.com/) is a good example of this. To find other companies offering free e-mail list management services, click on one of the links below:

- emailAddresses.com: http://www.emailaddresses.com/email_mailing.htm

- The Free Country: http://www.thefreecountry.com/webmaster/freeemail.shtml

- EPDigest.com: http://epdigest.com/resources/management/freehosting/

Your Internet Service Provider may also provide disk space and free list management capabilities. Many ISPs offer either "Majordomo" or "Listserve" as a free service to their subscribers. Functionality will vary with the ISP, so contact yours to see if list management is an option and what capabilities are included.

Explore these alternatives and pick the one that works best for your situation. Or, as you will learn in the next chapters, for a small price you can circumvent the above drawbacks by purchasing list management software for your desktop PC or else subscribing to an online service.

Free Desktop List Management Software

If you prefer to manage everything from your desktop, check out Pegasus Mail at www.pmail.com. It is **FREE** software that can be downloaded and installed on your PC. Pegasus Mail offers a host of useful features, including extensive security, MailMerge and basic list management functions.

Another **FREE** package, GroupMail (http://www.infacta.com/gm.asp), offers many desirable features, including subscription management, personalization, and the ability to send HTML email.

WorldMerge is another good product. It contains a (WYSIWYG) HTML editor plug-in which allows you to visually edit HTML emails. The package is helpful in sending a customized newsletter to subscribers, as well as personalized "thank you" e-mail to your new clients. A **FREE** evaluation copy of WorldMerge can be downloaded at the ColoradoSoft Website: http://www.coloradosoft.com/worldmrg/index.htm.

Finally, check out the shareware version of Gammadyne's Mail software (http://gammadyne.com/mmail.htm#html). This **FREE** version has some limitations, but the package overall is an excellent solution for bulk e-mail handling and includes many sophisticated features.

Archive Your Newsletters

Archive past issues of your newsletter on your website or hard drive. These are a valuable resource. If you have a Website, you can motivate new sign-ups by granting them access to articles contained in previous issues. Some articles can even be periodically recycled. Even if you do not have a Website, you can offer your clients a digest of previous articles that they can request from you.

Manage Your Marketing Campaign

In addition to list management, there are several advanced functions exist to assist you in effective client communication, managing your campaign and tracking the progress of your efforts. These are not likely to be found in "free" software available on the Web, but are extremely helpful and amplify your productivity. Let's take a moment to familiarize ourselves with these useful tools, as they are integral to the desktop software applications covered in the next chapter:

Function	Description
Autoresponder	Autoresponders let you prepare (in advance) a series of e-mail messages to clients which are then delivered based on either actions taken by a client or according to a schedule…or both. The objectives are to automate timely correspondence and maintain periodic, regular contact with clients. In short, it is a "hands free" productivity tool that allows you to be responsive and attentive to your clients. Timely communication with clients is key to successful sales. For example, suppose a recipient of your newsletter clicks on a link to see your other listings or mortgage programs that are located on your Website. This can be detected, and an automated, personalized e-mail sent to the reader later that day thanking him for his inquiry and offering to answer any questions he may have or to assist him in finding (or funding) a new home. In addition to automatically handling follow-up e-mails, autoresponders allow you to schedule prepared e-mails for periodic delivery according to any frequency you may want to set and to any select groups of clients. A sequence of compelling e-mails can be established for new prospects, for instance. In other words, you can "drip, drip, drip" reinforcing messages to clients that enhance your position as the person who is best equipped to assist them in their real estate needs. Because of their ability to automate repetitive communications to clients, autoresponders are powerful tools that can dramatically boost your sales.

Function	Description
Tracking and Reporting	As the number of customers and prospects grows, it becomes difficult to track what was sent to whom and when. How many new subscribers do you have? When did they sign up? How many have you lost? Perhaps you should schedule a follow-up e-mail to them. What is the "click through" rate on links in your newsletter? Are your e-mail "bounces" increasing? Also, what does your sales pipeline look like? This information is helpful in improving your newsletter, managing your prospect database, and ultimately making more sales.
Targeting Specific Prospects	Based on the nature of your clients, you may want to segment them into different groups for more effective sales communications. For example, dividing your subscriber list into new prospects and past customers allows you to better prepare targeted e-mail correspondence. Notifying prospective buyers of a new listing or targeting homeowners with appreciated equity are two examples of how this capability can be beneficial.

On to the Next Chapter!

With these advanced functions fresh in mind, the next chapter shows you how reasonably-priced desktop software provides integrated solutions to handle newsletter and e-mail communications. Can you create, launch and conduct e-mail newsletter and marketing campaigns just using Microsoft Office and free Web downloads? Yes, but it can be cumbersome and requires a degree of technical awareness to make diverse software packages work together. Depending on your finances and the number of clients you have, it might be better to spend a little money to get an integrated solution that also enhances your productivity.

8. USING DESKTOP SOFTWARE TO CREATE AND DISTRIBUTE YOUR NEWSLETTERS

Thus far, we have learned how to create and distribute text- and graphically-based newsletters using Microsoft Word and Outlook, optionally supplemented by free list management software downloaded off the Web.

As you have seen, this involves creating and moving information among several applications – Word, Outlook and possibly third-party software. This is a good way to "test the waters" if your client list is small, if you're strapped for funds, or if you're just getting started in real estate.

This chapter takes you to the next level. Here, several excellent software applications that can run on your desktop PC to help you create, launch and manage your e-mail newsletters are identified and reviewed. These applications enhance your productivity by reducing the time and effort required for such activities.

The selection criteria for each application are: 1) Is it a reputable vendor with widely accepted software, 2) Is it compatible with Microsoft outlook, and 3) Is it relatively "cheap?" Some of the software handles only one or two functions, while others offer a fully integrated solution. You can choose which best satisfies your needs and pocketbook.

Use Inexpensive Web Authoring Software to Create HTML E-Mail Newsletters

As seen in the last chapter, graphical e-mail newsletters can be created using Microsoft Word in a Web view mode then saving the results as a "Web Page, Filtered" document (which takes out unique Word attributes and makes your HTML newsletter more universally acceptable to major e-mail applications). Free downloads from the Web were also identified to assist in the creation of a newsletter. Important among these are WYSIWYG HTML editors that can assist you in modifying newsletter templates.

Ideally, you should have a Website or simply storage space on a Web server where you can maintain images and reference them. Fortunately, today it costs very little to "rent" storage space on a Web server. Several ISPs offer simple Websites that can store your images for just a few dollars monthly. And although you do not have to do so, these Website vendors offer easy-to-use tools that let you to create straightforward Websites a well. The next chapter explores this subject further, identifying several low-priced hosting vendors that can help you to launch your own Website.

For now, let's concentrate on how you can easily create pure HTML newsletters. If you want to take advantage of wizards and software that are specifically designed to help you produce professional-looking graphical Web pages for the purpose of using them as an e-mail newsletter, then purchasing an inexpensive Web authoring package is the answer.

On the next page, you will find a summary of several inexpensive Web authoring applications and one publishing package. Each supports the creation of HTML Web pages that can be used for e-mail newsletters. Some vendors even provide Web space for storing images online. Details about these solutions and others can be found in Appendix 1.

Use Inexpensive List Management Software to Effectively Manage Distribution and Internet Marketing

With a small expense, you can purchase one of several low-priced, fully-integrated solutions that provide advanced e-mail list management capabilities. Some even offer free or low-priced Web space for storing your newsletter images.3 Many software packages also include metrics and tracking reports so that you can quickly and easily gauge the success of your newsletter.

All the reviewed packages on the next page are compatible with Microsoft Outlook, making it easy to import your existing contact lists and use Outlook to accomplish a variety of customized e-mail marketing campaigns. The productivity gains you will reap from any of these packages far outweighs the small expense. Detailed information about each application can be found in Appendix 2.

---

[3] This allows your newsletter to "reference" an image from a Website, using an invisible link in your HTML-based e-mail. Your clients see only the intended photo or clipart. Referenced images circumvent most formatting problems with recipients who have non-Microsoft e-mail applications (e.g., AOL or Lotus Notes), result in smaller sized e-mails and take less bandwidth to transmit.

Chapter 8: Using Desktop Software to Create and Distribute your Newsletters

Figure 1. Desktop PC HTML Newsletter & Web Authoring Software

Features	Boomerang Software Webpage Creation Kit (www.boomerangsoftware.com)	High Impact eMail 2.0 (www.templatezone.com)	Microsoft Publisher (www.microsoft.com/office/publisher)	MicroVision WebExpress 3.0 (www.mvd.com/webexpress)	Splash Web Author (www.101ware.com/splash/free_resources)	SJ Namo WebEditor6 Suite (www.jr.com)	VCOM WebEasy (www.v-com.com)	VisualVision Easy Web Editor (www.easywebeditor.com)	Virtual Mechanics SiteSpinner v2 (www.virtualmechanics.com/index.html)	Web Studio 4.0 (www.webstudio.com)
Easy to Use	✓	✓	✓	✓	✓	✓	✓	✓	✓	✓
WYSIWYG[1] HTML Editor	✓	✓	✓	✓	✓	✓		✓	✓	✓
Templates	✓	✓	✓	✓	✓	✓	✓	✓	✓	
Wizards[2]	✓	✓	✓							✓
Tutorial	✓		✓	✓	✓	✓	✓	✓	✓	✓
Instruction Manual	✓	✓	✓							✓
Publishing Tool[3]	✓	✓	✓	✓	✓	✓	✓	✓	✓	✓
Image Mapper[4]	✓		✓	✓		✓	✓	✓	✓	✓
Free Technical Support	✓	✓	✓	✓				✓	✓	✓
Download Software Price	$ 59.95	$ 49.95	$120-160	$ 69.95	$ 19.95	$ 69.99	$ 29.95	$ 59.90	$ 49.00	$ 89.99

[1] "What You See Is What You Get". A WYSIWYG editor allows you to visually create Webpages or HTML newsletters (which are essentially Webpages inserted into an e-mail body) without having to understand complex coding procedures.

[2] A Wizard guides you through the complex tasks to create and publish Webpages, such as adding banners or interactive processes.

[3] One of the most difficult things to learn about web publishing is 'uploading' the Web pages prepared on your desktop to a computer that "host" your Website. Publishing Tools mask the complexity of this operation by automatically accomplishing uploads.

[4] An "image mapper" allows you to set boundaries within an image and place links in each area.

Figure 2. Desktop PC List Management Software

Features	Act! Version 6.0 for 2004 www.act.com	Anconia RocketSales www.anconia.com	AY Software AY Mailer 2.3 Professional www.aysoft.com	Bluelark Newsletter Pro www.bluelark.com	Desktop Server 4 http://www.kaxy.com/desktop_server_4_specs_and_bulk_email_software_and_address_lists_for_opt_in_spam.htm	EXP Elite www.extractorpro.com	Gammadyne Mailer http://gammadyne.com/mmail.htm?ref=10088	Mach5 Mailer www.mach5.com	Maillist King (Standard) www.xequte.com/maillisting	MAPILab Subscription Manager & Send Personality www.mapilab.com	Sprika LiteMail 2.2 www.sprika.com	4OfficeAutomation EmailUnlimiterd 6.0 www.4officeautomation.com	WriteExpress - High Impact www.writeexpress.com/hi/high-impact-email.htm
Compatible with Microsoft Outlook	✓	✓	✓			✓	✓	✓	✓	✓	✓	✓	
Includes HTML Newsletter Templates	✓	✓	✓									✓	
WYSIWYG HTML Editor	✓	✓	✓								✓		
Handles Text, HTML and Multi-Part (Text & HTML) Formats	✓		✓	✓		✓	✓	✓	✓	✓			
Requires Website	✓	✓	✓										
Offers Web-based space for your photos, etc.												✓	
Build a Series of Autoresponders			✓	✓	✓	✓	✓	✓		✓	✓		
Automatic Opt-In Subscription Registration	✓	✓	✓	✓	✓	✓	✓	✓	✓	✓			
Automatically Handles Unsubscribe	✓	✓	✓	✓	✓	✓	✓	✓	✓	✓			
Confirmations (for Opt-In & Unsubscribe)	✓	✓		✓	✓	✓	✓	✓					
Bounced E-Mail Handling	✓	✓	✓	✓	✓	✓	✓				✓		
Targeted Sending to Specific Contact Criteria	✓	✓	✓	✓	✓	✓	✓	✓					
Personalization (Custom Fields)	✓	✓	✓	✓	✓	✓	✓	✓			✓		
Tracking and Reporting	✓	✓	✓	✓	✓	✓	✓				✓		
Built-In Spam Checker	✓					✓	✓						
Contact Database	✓	✓		✓			✓						
Includes Generic E-Mail Templates (e.g., Stationary and Forms)	✓	✓										✓	✓
Free Technical Support	✓	✓	✓	✓	✓	✓	✓	✓					
Download Software Price	$ 229.95	$ 149.00	$139.95	$ 99.00	$ 299.00	$ 149.00	$ 99.95 / $49.00	$ 99.95 / $49.00	$ 24.00	$ 20.00	$ 197.00	$ 49.95	

9. AN ALTERNATE APPROACH – USE OUTSOURCE SERVICES

Thus far, you have learned how e-mail newsletters can be produced and managed using your desktop PC. We have also discussed the merits of having a Website and looked at some low-priced tools and hosting venders to accomplish this.

Doing your own newsletter takes work, time, and a willingness to learn new skills. There is also a minimal level of technical competence necessary to tackle the self-preparation and publishing of a newsletter. The upside, of course, is that you can prepare and manage e-mail newsletters for very little cost if you are willing to contribute the time and effort to do so.

Maybe it just seems like too much trouble to you. While you want to put out a newsletter, you also want to avoid adding software to your PC and learning how to use it. Maybe your funds are limited now, or you don't feel comfortable investing in desktop software before knowing whether an e-mail newsletter is going to work for you. Besides, your company or agency already has a Website, and you enjoy a separate page with a distinct URL (i.e., Web address) within that Website. There has to be an easier way to enjoy the benefits of having an e-mail newsletter rather than doing the whole thing yourself. Right?

Right. If you are willing to pay for the benefit, several outsource services exist that will prepare, deliver and manage your e-mail newsletter. Fees aside, it is still much easier to use an outsourced solution like this to satisfy your newsletter needs. Typically, these services require an annual or monthly fee to perform the following functions:

- Preparation of some or all of the content
- Insertion of your name, photo and contact information into a standard monthly newsletter template
- Delivery of the newsletter to an e-mail list provided by you
- Management of the e-mail list (subscribe, unsubscribe, bounced e-mails, etc.)
- Reporting metrics and statistics about the success of your e-mail campaign

Another advantage to using an outsource service is that you can access it from anywhere over the Internet. You will have your own password-protected account on the provider's Website. There, you can store your distribution list and use vendor-supplied tools to create your newsletter.

Chapter 9: An Alternate Approach – Use Outsource Services

Completely outsourcing your newsletter preparation and management usually results in getting your newsletter off the ground sooner. Things run smoother too. In many cases, you don't have to deal with the monthly or quarterly "chore" of preparing a newsletter. All e-mail list management functions are performed for you. In short, it is an easy way to keep in front of your clients with minimal effort.

The outsource service providers presented later in this chapter under the heading "For Realtors" will do most of the work for you. They offer the simplest answer to launching an e-mail newsletter. Of course, you must be prepared to pay more for a complete service that does just about everything for you than for one where you are still primarily responsible for creating the newsletter.

Even with a complete service, you still have to do some work. Foremost, you must gather opt-in e-mail addresses, either through your Website or by solicitations within your territory. You may also want to contribute relevant articles related to local issues.

The downside of using an outside service to completely handle your e-mail newsletter is that you lose flexibility in being able to design the newsletter to suit your individual purposes. Mostly, the newsletter is a boilerplate format that allows a few custom inserts. You have little say over the type and number of links in your newsletter or the content material.

In contrast to those who do everything for you, there are a full spectrum of generic outsource services available at reduced pricing. If you are willing to create your newsletter using online templates and easy-to-understand tools, you can save a bundle of money AND have a superior newsletter designed to your preferences. Those services presented in the table labeled "General E-Mail Newsletter Outsource Services" are all reasonably priced and offer tools and aids to assist you in preparing, launching and managing a newsletter designed by yourself.

Whatever course you select, be sure to shop around first. In addition to pricing, compare the outsource services by features and ease of use. Visit their Websites to learn more about the services. Try a free trial from one or more of the online services to see how well they work for you and whether the generated newsletter satisfies your objectives. Also investigate what type of support you will receive if you have any problems. It pays to take a little time to explore each candidate before making a final selection.

From an economic standpoint, outsource services are initially less expensive compared to purchasing software for your desktop or Website. That is what makes them attractive. Nonetheless, since you have to keep paying a fee to use them, outsource services ultimately cost more than acquiring software to do the same thing. But to many, this extra cost is offset by their "hassle free" nature. Money aside, outsource services are an easy answer for sending out periodic e-mail newsletters.

A final note – most outsource service providers will give a ten percent (or more) discount if you sign up for an annual contract and pay in advance. The alternative is to pay on a month-to-month basis, which allows you to discontinue the service at any time. The best choice for you should reflect your commitment to using e-mail newsletters as a marketing tool.

Examine the outsource service choices available on the next pages. Determine which best satisfies your needs while fitting your pocketbook.

Table 6. Outsource E-Mail Newsletter Services Targeting Realtors

---

NewsRoute   www.newsroute.info/RealEstate/Index.htm

- Offers customized eNewsletters for Realtors with topics of interest to homeowners, handy resources and ability to insert premier listings.

- Helps companies set up and manage their email Communications Program. Manage your email lists, merge and personalize mailings, and manage the "back end" work that goes with any successful marketing program. Helps you track responses so that you know if you are missing the mark or hitting the target.

- List management services include initial analysis, de-duping and loading of the database. Ongoing services include backup, list integrity and analysis.

- Offer consulting services as well.

Realty Times   http://realtytimes.com/

- Leading Real Estate News site on the Internet. Nearly half a million consumers and Real Estate professionals come to Realty Times each month.

- Offers Agent Publicity Package with flyers, x-links on 50 sites, website content, monthly personalized (photo & contact info) newsletter with premium content; any articles contributed by you get exposure on 50 websites.

- Auto-Emailer system automatically sends out your HTML-based Real Estate Update Newsletter on the date of your choosing

- Pricing:

    o   Agent Publicity Package: $999 per year

    o   Real Estate Update (Newsletter only): $299 per year ($24.92 monthly); charges another $299 for printable version

    o $50 set-up fee, plus $10 monthly for Auto-Emailer system

---

Touchpoint Communications   http://www.touchpointcom.com/

- Offers personalized marketing newsletters

- The newsletter is emailed to you in PDF format. You then e-mail it from your own computer. It has four pages with personalization on the front and back. You may supply a color photo and logo. Touchpoint does all changes for free and you can opt to write you own articles with each issue. They will typeset your article for free!

- Pricing:

    o   Pricing is based on a personalized assessment of your needs.

Table 7. General E-Mail Newsletter Outsource Services

Bronto   http://bronto.com/segments/newsletter/

- Integrates into your Website; easy to use
- Easily send out a webpage (or text, HTML, template) for your newsletter
- Create surveys and forms
- Save time with automated and comprehensive list management functions
- Includes automatic confirmation e-mails for new subscribers
- Target your mailing with sophisticated segmentation tools
- Track opens, forwards, click-throughs, undeliverables and much more
- Extensive support
- Pricing:
    - Depends on the number of contacts
    - $100/month for up to 1,000 contacts

Click-N-Drop   www.clickndrop.com

- Tools and features make designing, building and launching an assortment of professional online /email marketing campaigns and programs fast, simple and effective.
- Customizable user options let you automatically control, manage and maintain list, optimize email formatting, and meet email compliance regulations.
- Detailed summary and granular, tracking, monitoring, reporting and charting lets you test, analyze and mine data, providing the intelligence you need improve marketing performance and better identify and target best prospects
- Create, manage and deploy professional newsletters in minutes, without any HTML or programming knowledge or newsletter building experience.
- Create, manage and deploy professional surveys, contests, opt-in and client profile update forms in minutes.
- Create, manage and deploy professional polls from your newsletters or web site in minutes.
- The fastest way to manage your press releases electronically. Post them, send them and manage them within your website without any HTML or programming skills. It's fully integrated with our Email Blaster, and is the best way to disseminate your press releases to investors, media and customers and track who's seeing and noticing your news.
- An assortment of creative turn-key tools and pre-designed templates make it easy to launch a variety of powerful, proven and tested online/email marketing programs, activities and campaigns.
- Pricing for *eCommunicator Pro*:
    - $29.95 monthly for up to 5,000 e-mails. Additional licenses for only $10 monthly can share the 5,000/month e-mail limit.
    - $2.50 for each additional 1,000 emails per month.

Table 7. (Continued)

Constant Contact   http://www.constantcontact.com/index.jsp?cc=

- Constant Contact®, Do-It-Yourself Email Marketing™ helps small and mid-sized businesses and associations develop an ongoing relationship with their customers and site visitors. Constant Contact makes it easy and affordable to build and manage permission-based email lists, create and send eye-catching HTML email newsletters, announcements and promotions, and track email campaign results.
- Builds and manages permission email lists of all sizes
- Wizards and over 75 customizable HTML email templates (or start from scratch)
- Measures email campaign results instantly
- 100% web-based and no technical skill required
- CAN-SPAM Act compliant
- High email deliverability
- Affordable monthly pricing
- Pricing:
  - FREE for 0-50 e-mails per month
  - $10 monthly for 51-250 e-mails
  - $25 monthly for 251-2,500 e-mails
  - 60-day free trial

GraphicMail   http://email.about.com/cs/marketingasprevs/gr/graphicmail.htm

- E-mail marketing and newsletter application service provider.   Enter addresses by hand, import from csv files or use a ready-made HTML signup form.   Offers a WYSIWYG HTML editor, and lets you edit the HTML source and a plain text version.
- Includes newsletter templates and lets you create your own reusable templates, too.
- Automatically handles bounced addresses and un-subscribes; creates open rate statistics.
- You can collect and store subscriber information and use it for personalization in mailings.
- Click-through statistics on the link level.
- Mailings can be scheduled up to one month in advance.
- Supports Internet Explorer 5/6 and Windows 98/ME/NT/2000/3/XP.
- Pricing:
  - $9.95/monthly for up to 2,000 e-mails per month
  - $19.95 annually for up to 2,000 e-mails; $49.95 for up to 10,000 e-mails per year.

Table 7. (Continued)

HTML Email Marketing   http://www.html-email-marketing.com/

- Create newsletters from more than 50 ready-to-use templates
- Flexible template customize capabilities allow you to easily change the message, company logo, product image, font, size, color and links to your web site
- Customized newsletter service also available
- Import your own HTML newsletter creations
- Auto-Conversion HTML or text. Automatically deliver to HTML-compatible recipients or convert to the "clean" text email version
- Compatible with multiple email formats such as HTML, Text, AOL, Hotmail, Yahoo, Mac OS
- Run email newsletter campaigns from easy-to-use wizards
- Upload your list easily with one click, the upload utilities can import your list from Outlook, Excel, Access etc.
- Deliver to your target subscribers automatically
- Automatic list management for subscribed, unsubscribed, and bounced email addresses
- Track click-through responses, make it easy to take further steps with customers
- Pricing:
    - Starts at $9.95 monthly

IntelliContact   http://www.intellicontact.com/index.pl

- Industry-leading reporting system (statistics and metrics)
- A complete contact management and follow-up system
- Choose from our selection of sign up forms or create your own
- Complete bounce-back email handling
- Use mail-merge to send personalized HTML or TEXT email
- MessageBuilder™ to easily create professional HTML newsletters in a matter of minutes--without knowing any HTML. Select from their sample HTML templates or use your own
- Complete list add/remove/sent statistics and activity reports
- Easily import subscribers and contacts from any application or database
- Built in HTML Editor
- Fully searchable database for easy finding and updating of subscriber information
- Get preformatted HTML subscribe forms. Let users join your list from your Web site in seconds. Subscribers manage their profile to ensure you have accurate contact information. No more outdated email addresses.
- Pricing:
    - Up to 500 subscribers - $9.95/month or $107.46 annually
    - Up to 1,000 subscribers - $13.00/month or $140.40 annually
    - Up to 2,500 subscribers - $24.00/month or $259.20 annually

---

Table 7. (Continued)

isendit   http://www.isendit.com/isendit/email_broadcast.asp

- Personalization - Each email is individually addressed with the recipients' name and email address.
- List Management - Submit and maintain your recipient lists using our simple web interface. Your segmented lists can remain on our systems eliminating the need to constantly resend a list before each email broadcast.
- Scheduling - Choose a delivery time for your mass email communications. Stage complete email campaigns in advance.
- HTML or Text email - Easily create HTML emails. Text emails can be created on the fly by writing your message on our site or by copying and pasting it from existing content.
- Status Reporting - Online status reporting of your broadcast is available on-demand. All reports are downloadable to CSV for use with applications such as Microsoft Excel.
- Web based Interface - Create your broadcast using our friendly Web interface. No proprietary software is needed!
- Preview - Preview your communication in your web browser before approving you broadcast.
- Attachments - Any type of attachment is supported with no size restrictions. Up to 10 attachment files can be added to your html or text email.
- Retries - Emails are automatically retried for delivery when the recipient's mail servers is unavailable.
- Bounce Management - Optionally, your email bounces can be directed to an alternative email address.
- Pricing:
    o $.04 per e-mail

Microsoft List Builder   http://www.bcentral.com/products/lb/default.asp

- Create, deliver and track personalized e-mail marketing campaigns.
- Use their HTML templates to send professional e-mail newsletters and announcements, or import and send your own HTML messages.
- Use personalization features to address your e-mail recipients by name.
- Send targeted campaigns based on subscribers' demographic information.
- Track your e-mail marketing campaigns in real time to see how many recipients received, opened and clicked on links within your e-mail.
- Pricing:
    o $19.95 for Starter Package (30-Day free Trial; up to 1,000 e-mails monthly)
    o $199 annually
    o Optional Live support: $9.95/month or $99.95/year

10. WHY YOU SHOULD HAVE A WEBSITE!

It is difficult to do business today without a Website. First, prospective clients expect you to have a Website, simply as a matter of credibility. Second, a Website is where you have an opportunity to promote yourself and your products or services to your marketplace. If your competitors have a Website and you do not, then you suffer a significant competitive disadvantage.

E-mail newsletters are intended to be part of a robust marketing campaign, one purpose of which is to drive clients to your Website where they can be exposed to your products and services, learn more about your brokerage and you personally, view your listings, read customer testimonials, review your programs, participate in special promotions, see your press releases, read interesting industry information, or find out about upcoming trade shows or events. Even if your brokerage or company already has a Website, you should establish a personal site to cultivate your own clientele. At minimum, arrange to get a personal page on your broker's or company's Website to which you can refer customers and prospects.

Having a Website also facilitates the creation and management of e-mail newsletters. And, as you will see, it is possible to establish a personal Website for very little expense.

Creating and Managing E-Mail Newsletters is Easier with a Website

When HTML newsletters are sent via e-mail with embedded photos, clipart and other "objects," they are large in (storage) size, take longer to download from your ISP and use more space on the recipient's hard disk. A better – and the most common – way to create newsletters is to use "pure" HTML wherein photos, clipart and other image objects are downloaded from a Website to the recipient's PC when the e-mail is opened. Instead of embedding a photo, for example, within the e-mail newsletter itself, a reference or link (e.g., http://www.mywebsite.com/photo) to the photo is inserted. From the reader's standpoint, the result is the same – when he/she opens the e-mail containing your newsletter in its body, they see the photo is its proper location.

Figure 3. How "Linked" Graphics Work in a Newsletter

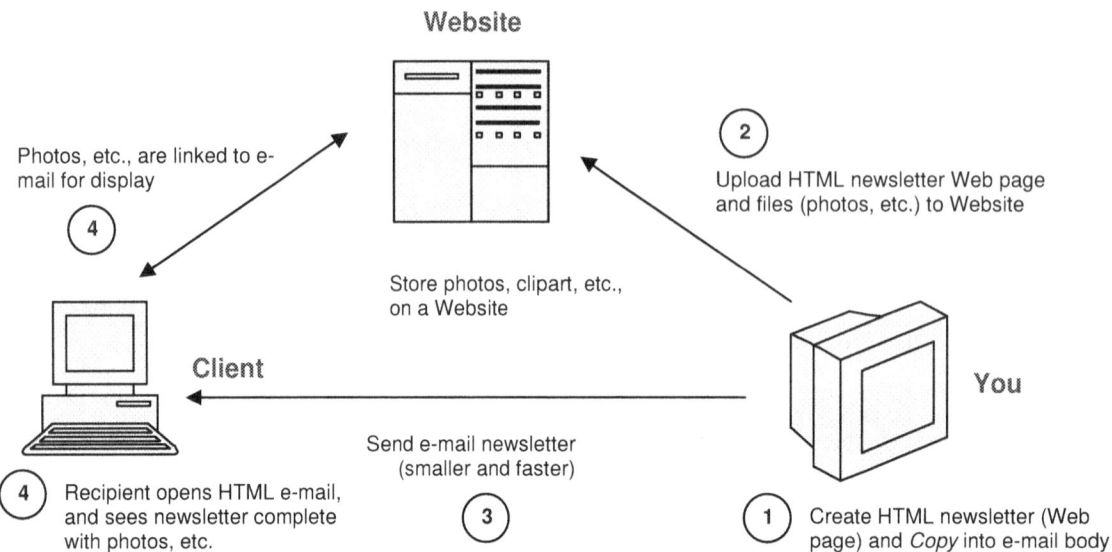

Your subscription list will grow faster if you have a Website. First, your exposure to a larger audience is ensured by a Website. Adding a "Click here to subscribe to a monthly newsletter" link to a Website that generates a subscription form is an easy, effective means of gaining new clients.

Websites are also the ideal location to conduct automated list management activities. It is much simpler to set up "subscribe" and "unsubscribe" functionalities on a Website. Most companies that provide hosting services for private Websites have predefined scripts that can be incorporated to handle these activities, automatically capturing the information you need for new subscribers and communicating "unsubscribe" data to resident list management software. List management activities can be easily accomplished by securely accessing your Website from anywhere through a Web browser such as Microsoft Explorer. Likewise, newsletters can be updated and sent directly from a Website. In short, Websites provide a central, readily accessible location from which all activities involved in managing a newsletter can be conducted.

With a Website, you can keep your newsletters brief and to the point, ensuring they are more likely to be opened and read. In effect, your HTML newsletter is reference guide. It highlights appealing stories and services, and then makes it easy for the reader to acquire additional information for areas of interest. Reader navigation and the ability to quickly find desired information are facilitated through hyperlinks to specific pages on a Website. And once a client has transferred to your Website, the odds are he/she will explore other areas of interest (such as your listings, mortgage programs, or an archived newsletter with a story about "Ten Things You Should Know Before Selling Your Home."

Alternatively, Host Your Newsletter on a Website

Website offer another option – the ability to publish your newsletter on the Website itself and direct subscribers to a specific Webpage to read it. Under this approach, your monthly or quarterly e-mail to subscribers simply includes a hyperlink to the Webpage. For example:

> Your monthly newsletter from ABC Realty is now ready and may be
> reviewed at www.abcrealty.com/newsletter.

Interested readers who click on this link have access to your newsletter and the rest of your Website. The main advantages and disadvantages of a Website-hosted newsletter are:

Pros	Cons
• Simpler; less work • More likely to circumvent spam blockers, since only a text message is sent to subscribers • Can track who visits your Website to read the newsletter	• Readership is likely to be less than that of a self-contained e-mail newsletter • Newsletter is less likely to be forwarded to friends, co-workers and relatives

Studies have shown that readership declines when an e-mail recipient must click on a link to go to a Website to read a newsletter. However, there is a positive benefit to maintaining current and archived newsletters on a Website as an inducement to recruit new subscribers.

Continuous Worldwide Exposure

Websites open the door to acquiring new business from outside your immediate locale. Someone in New York, for example, who is contemplating moving to San Diego might do an Internet search for local Realtors and visit your site. This presents a wonderful opportunity to gain a new client before they are exposed to the competition. Likewise, remote buyers and sellers may require a local service to arrange pre-approved financing, perform residential searches, or perhaps get an appraisal for property left to them in a will. Many Realtors report significant jumps in revenue after launching their Websites. The benefits of advertising one's services worldwide around the clock, every day of the year, cannot be overstated.

Detect Opportunities for Early Follow-up

Here's another benefit – Websites have metrics that report to you how many people have visited your site, which page they first viewed and how they traveled through their site. This will help you to fine tune your site to emphasize areas of indicated interest. Some metrics even provide the e-mail address of viewers. Wouldn't it be nice to know if someone in your geographical market was looking at articles about selling their home or visiting your listings? Promotional offers, such as "Click here to receive a free market value assessment," can be placed on relevant Web pages to capture new clients. Autoresponders can be constructed to automatically sent e-mails thanking registering visitors and offering your services. More so than many enterprises, capitalizing on timely opportunities is key to success in the real estate business.

Websites Are Now Easy to Prepare

You would be surprised how easy it is to create an impressive Website. Most people can now prepare simple Websites within a few hours. It has never been simpler to launch your own Website.

If you can use Microsoft Word, you can prepare a Website. Many Website hosting vendors now include templates and easy-to-use tools that help novices to quickly launch professionally-looking sites. These include "drag and drop" WYSIWYG HTML editors, canned routines and publishing aids accompanied by online tutorials. In addition, user-friendly software identified earlier allows you to create impressive Websites on your PC for subsequent uploading to an Internet Service Provider (ISP) where site hosting occurs.

It Doesn't Cost a Bundle to Have a Website!

The Internet has become a commodity service. Having a Website is no longer expensive, nor does it require mastering "black arts" to quickly begin advertising your services online. Many vendors, such as GeoCities, Hypermart and Xoom, offer free Website hosting in exchange for accompanying advertising on your Web pages. Others offer low-priced deals with no advertising. Most hosting vendors have packages ranging from personal Websites through business-oriented sites complete with online shopping carts.

The Internet Service provider who currently carries your e-mail account is a good place to start if you are looking for a Web host provider. Often, they offer these services and you can reduce your overall Internet bill by signing on with them to also host your business Website (using this new domain as your primary e-mail account). Sometimes, your e-mail account already provides 5-10MB of space for a personal Website intended to share photos, etc. – do not use this for real estate business without first consulting with your ISP. If your ISP seems like a feasible choice for a real estate Website, do the math and see how this alternative compares to overall pricing using one of the low-priced Web hosting services identified in this chapter.

Ideally, you should have an advertising-free Website (unless someone is paying you to host real-estate related ads). When purchasing a Web hosting account, two major items to consider are disk storage space and the data transfer rate (also called bandwidth). These are typically measured in Megabytes (MB) or Gigabytes (GB; about 1000 MB). Transfer rates are measured in GB/month.

For a typical Website, 1MB of storage accommodates 20-40 simple Web pages. Additional storage may be needed for list management and other applications. Fortunately, storage today is dirt cheap and not a major concerning in pricing Web hosting. Minimum recommended storage is 50MB to provide room for expansion, and at least 10GB/month bandwidth. Some other account features to examine are:

- The number of e-mail addresses you will receive and any special forms of e-mail delivery
- Various management tools, like control panels and traffic analyzers
- The level of customer support for technical assistance
- Special components included, such as templates, user-friendly development tools, special extensions, and "canned" scripts or routines
- Miscellaneous features, like a free Internet marketing kit

Carefully evaluate a potential hosting vendor on the merits of its site preparation tools and whether you feel comfortable using them. Ideally, the vendor should offer easily modified templates and step-by-step instructions or a "wizard" to assist you.

Of course, you want to be sure that the vendor selected offers the ability to handle newsletter subscriptions. You must be able to easily create a subscription form that is launched when a Website visitor clicks on a relevant link (e.g., "Click here to sign up for my newsletter"). The information collected in the form will be e-mailed to you for follow-up action. You can store this in your PC-based mailing list or forward it to a mail list vendor for updating your database. In the latter case, the information can even be e-mailed directly to the vendor for automated action. Better yet, the link on your site takes the visitor to your list management vendor where they sign up directly, never aware that they have left your Website.

You must also register an Internet domain name ($10-$20). This is the special Internet address (Universal Resource Locator, or "URL") that uniquely identifies your Website's location (such as, janesrealty.com). Most Web hosting vendors can provide this service for you at the same time that you sign up for an account with them.

The chart on the next page summarizes a few of the reputable low-cost Web host vendors, comparing the features and pricing of each. Although each offers a variety of tools, you are usually better off purchasing a low-priced Web authoring tool, developing Web pages on your desktop and uploading the results to your Website. However, first-time Website developers may want to stick with the vendor-provided tools for simplicity. Carefully scrutinize the line entitled "Web Tools" to gain insight into what type of solution will work best for you:

- "Included" means that the vendor provides templates and a set of easy-to-use tools that let you customize the logo, text, photos and background colors. These tools typically allow you to track the number of visitor visiting your site, etc., as well. This is the best solution if you have no experience in creating Websites and do not want to invest the time and effort to learn how to use a Web authoring product like Microsoft FrontPage.

- If you wish to learn or already know how to use a Web authoring product, then Website hosting vendors that only support FTP uploads may be best for you, as they typically offer more sophisticated features to their customers.

Those who want an "all in one" solution for creating a simple Website with an e-mail marketing solution, and don't mind paying more, may want to explore the Geocities/Yahoo solution.

Figure 4. Low-Priced Web Hosting Vendors

Hosting Vendor	Apollo Total Solutions Shared (Basic) www.apollohosting.com	AvaHost Plus plan www.avahost.net	Geocities/Yahoo Starter Package geocities.yahoo.com	Globat.com www.globat.com/	iPowerWeb Businesspro www.ipowerweb.com/	Lunarpages Shuttle Plan www.lunarpages.com	Register.com www.register.com	StartLogic Pro Logic www.startlogic.com/index.html
Disk Storage Space	400MB	400MB	50MB	2000MB	800MB	800MB	50MB+	1000MB
Transfer Bandwidth (GB/Month)	10GB	20GB	20GB	60GB	40GB	40GB	3GB+	40GB
# E-Mail Accounts	50	100	10	2000	400	Unlimited	Unlimited	Unlimited
# E-Mail Autoresponders	Unlimited	$100.00	None	$100.00	Unlimited	$29.99/Yr.	None	Unlimited
Web Mail	Included	Included	No	Included	Included	Included	Optional	Included
Domain Name Registration ($/Yr.)	$15.00	$9.95	Free	$12.00	Free or $20.00	$14.95	$20.00	$20.00
# Sub-domains (e.g., subtopic.domain.com)[1]	Yes	35	10	35	10	15	?	10
Website Traffic Statistics	Included	Included	No	Included	Included	Included	Included	Included
Account Control Panel[2]	Included	Included	Included	Included	Included	Included	Included	Included
Web Content[3]	Included	Included	Optional	Included	Included		Included	Included
Web Tools[4]	FTP Only	FTP Only	Included	FTP Only	FTP Only	FTP Only	Included	Included
# Mailing Lists Supported	Unlimited	$10.00	$10/Mo.	?	Yes	?	?	?
Search Engine Submission[5]	Yes	Yes	Chargeable	$49.95/Yr.	Yes	Yes	Yes	Yes
Customer Support	Phone & Internet	Phone & Internet	Phone & Internet	Internet-Based	Phone & Internet	Phone & Internet	Phone & Internet	Phone & Internet
Set-Up Fee	Free	Free	Free	39.95	Free	Free	Free	Free
Annual Price (1 Year may be due in advance)	$15.96/Mo.	$9.25/Mo.	$11.95/Mo.	$7.50/Mo.	$7.95/Mo.	$7.95/Mo.	$4.95/Mo.+	$7.50/Mo.

[1] Sub-domains are Web pages with dedicated materials, such as your listings, which can be referenced from a newsletter or other links.

[2] For management of the Website.

[3] Newsfeeds, etc, that can be used to add interesting content to your site.

[4] Templates, newsletter management, editors, etc.; "FTP Only" means you must create your Website using an HTML editor or a product like MS FrontPage and then upload it to your Website account.

[5] Submits your Website to the major search engines, such as Yahoo and Google, so that people can find you on the Internet.

Some hosting vendors offer Website templates designed especially for real estate agents. These easily modified templates can save you a lot of time. If this is what you are looking for, some to evaluate are:

Table 8. Websites with Real Estate Agent Templates

- RealtyDrive.com (http://www.realtydrive.com/): $9.95 monthly; free domain name; canned templates. Inquire about newsletter support.

- LinkURealty (http://www.linkusystems.com/realty/default.asp?source=google.com): $103 startup costs plus $29.99 monthly; supports customization.

- AgentNet (http://www.blitzdevelopment.com/agentnet_features.php): $150 start-up fee; $50 monthly or $500 annually. Sophisticated Website creation – database driven with video tour capability.

- MacroRealtor (http://www.macrorealtor.com/): $99 set-up fee plus $19.95 monthly.

- Real Estate Ready (www.realestateready.com): $9.99 startup fee plus $9.99 monthly. Limited to 5 pages; no e-mail accounts; content primarily limited to online listings display. Inquire about newsletter support.

- Point2Agent (http://agent.point2.com/): Free Website creation; multiple good templates; easy personalization of colors and graphics; 5 e-mail accounts; no credit card required. Standard free package includes third-party advertising. $29.95/month gives more listings, e-mail newsletter (autoresponder) system, referral areas, etc. Sophisticated Website.

If you are planning on doing an e-mail newsletter, be sure to confirm that the hosting vendor can and will support this! Make sure that whatever list management solution you intend to use is compatible with the hosting vendor's capabilities.

Alternatively, if you are willing and able to invest more money in a Website designed to meet your real estate goals, check out http://www.moneymakingwebsites.com/ where a personal consultant will assist you through the process.

Software for Your Website

Having a Website opens the door to running e-mail management software that is not available or practical for your desktop PC. It is also more productive to implement e-mail newsletter delivery and management at the Web level. Centralizing your e-mail activities on a Website allows you to manage these resources from anywhere. Moreover, installing software on your Website rather than on your desktop maximizes its benefits because everyone in the company (or real estate office) can utilize the same software. When the software cost and upkeep is amortized over several people, its expense becomes very low indeed.

Web-based software for e-mail newsletter management actually runs on a Web server, which is the online computer or vendor service that hosts your Website. It is hidden from Website visitors and accessible only through passwords available to you and others in your office who may share use of the software.

E-mail list management is a typical software function that runs on a Web server, providing automated support for Subscribe, Un-Subscribe, list management, newsletter delivery and archiving, autoresponders and a variety of other useful functions. Be advised, however, that adding software to your Website is not a recommended pursuit for those lacking a degree of technical acumen. However, your Website administrator or hosting vendor can assist (or even accomplish) the software installation. If you are using a hosting vendor for your Website, consult them first for recommended e-mail list management solutions.

If you and your associates are considering sharing the expense of a group newsletter solution, one low-cost software package that you may wish to consider is NewsletterPro4. This package handles list management functionality and runs on your office Website:

BlueLark NewsletterPro   www.bluelark.com

$99 one-time fee for single-user license; free installation, upgrades and support. $449 for 5 licenses; $849 for ten licenses. Free installation, upgrades and support.

NewsletterPro (v1.1) is newsletter management software for businesses that are looking for an affordable, yet powerful group emailing solution that is backed by powerful tracking and subscriber management features and is accessible via a web browser.

Key Features
- Easy-to-use, intuitive HTML administration interface allows you to administer the product from any location with web access.
- Built-in system of confirmed Opt-In verification by e-mail to verify the validity of the user's email address and to prevent malicious subscribers.
- Text, HTML and Multi-part MIME email formats are supported.
- Easy Importing of CSV formatted address book entries to the online address book, along with easy exporting to Excel from the online address book.
- An inbuilt option to include a Click-To link within the newsletter allows the user to customize/manage his subscription.
- Advanced Tracking options – both user and bounced email tracking – coupled with highly customizable reporting formats.
- Supports an unlimited number of Newsletter Lists, and Newsletters.

---

[4] Verbiage is a summary of that used on vendor's Website.

Helpful Hints for Setting Up Your Website

If you select any of the Website hosting vendors listed in this chapter, they will provide you with a set of easy-to-use tools and templates to assist you in creating your content. Be sure the one you select offers extensive Help features and (ideally) tutorials. They should also provide a user-friendly File Transfer Protocol (FTP) software interface for easy uploading of Web pages created on your own PC, photos, clipart, text, etc.

If this is your first Website, you are better off using the tools provided by the hosting vendor to create it. That way, if you encounter a problem or have a question, they can assist you. The Frequently Asked Questions (FAQ's) on the vendor's site provide a plethora of helpful hints and problem resolutions as well.

Once your Website is completed (you can modify it at any time), the key to success is to gain recognition form the major search engines. The top search engines account for 95% of Web traffic combined; Google, Yahoo!, AltaVista, Excite, Infoseek, HotBot, Lycos and WebCrawler. Here are some key things to remember:

- Choose a URL for each Webpage (i.e., your Website address) that has meaning because search engines scrutinize this. For example, if you are a Realtor whose farm is located in north Austin, then a good address might be www.north-austin-real-estate.com. When someone searches for real estate in north Austin, guess who's Website will be returned near the top of the heap?

- Your hosting vendor will provide a tool for you to set up "Meta Tags." These contain the Title of your Website and the keywords that search engines peruse their quest to match the search words entered by person performing the search. The "Title" for each page of your Website should be relevant to its content and use words that users are likely to be searching for. The keywords entered play a major part in determining your search engine ranking. So, make sure you enter keywords here (each separated by a space) that home buyers and sellers are likely to use when doing an Internet search. Also, check out competitor Websites that score high on search engine returns – after bringing up their Website, look at their Home Page text to see what keyword are used. While still on the Home Page, within your Internet browser, go to *View* and select *Source*. Near the top, you will see:

<meta name=keywords content="xxxx,yyyy,zzzz">

What lies between the parentheses are the keywords scrutinized for relevance by search engines. If these are helping your competitor to achieve a good ranking, they may work for you too.

- Your hosting vendor will also provide a tool to submit your Website to the major Internet search engines. It may be several days or even weeks before your information is indexed by a search engine, so give it time and don't be discouraged if you do not see instant results.

- Another secret to gaining recognition among search engines is to include keywords in the text on your opening ("Home") page, as most engines today also scan this page for matching verbiage.

- Many search engines, like Google, partially base your website ranking on the number of links coming into it. So, it pays to get complimentary sites (e.g., your Brokerage Website, local Board of Realtors site, sites listing local real estate agents, etc.) to install a descriptive link to your Website. Providing free articles for real estate publications that include a link to your Website works, as does doing online press releases (with your Website link included).

- Get your website listed in the major Internet directories: Yahoo! Directory (www.yahoo.com), Open Directory Project (www.dmoz.com), Google's search tool (www.froogle.com), www.about.com, and www.business.com[5]. Also be sure to get your site listed in any real estate directories, local and national.

- To avoid being tagged as a spammer by some search engines, do not:

    ✓ Use white text against a dark background
    ✓ Embed text within background colors
    ✓ Have duplicate pages on your Website, or
    ✓ Submit your website to search engines more than once monthly

Many hosting vendors have marketing guides you can access. Be sure to read this before creating your Website.

---

[5]Those considering putting up a personal Website for marketing real estate will benefit by exploring www.wilsonweb.com and perhaps signing up for a newsletter subscription.

11. WHAT IS THE BEST CHOICE FOR ME?

Now that you have learned the alternatives to creating your own e-mail newsletter, it is time to address the ultimate question: "Which is the best choice for me?" And that is exactly what we'll do in this chapter.

Only you can decide which course of action best suits your talents, time, preferences and pocketbook. And it is important that you be honest with yourself. Otherwise, you will get overextended, and your newsletter may never get off the ground or else could lose its momentum.

This chapter pulls everything together by first providing an objective means to assess your profile. It then offers one or more approaches to satisfy your situation. Each plan draws on materials covered in previous chapters. This approach provides a framework from which you can formulate a final plan that best suits your unique requirements.

Six Feasible Approaches to Launching and Managing an E-Mail Newsletter Campaign

Let us begin by defining six feasible approaches to designing, launching and managing your e-mail campaign. These are referred to as Plans A through G, and each may be implemented by itself or in conjunction with other Plans. They cover the full spectrum of skills, effort and resources. Each Plan assumes that you at least have - or have access to - a PC or Macintosh and are prepared to invest some time and effort to have an ongoing newsletter campaign.

The Plans are modular in nature and may be combined in certain configurations to align with your goals and capabilities, as you will see once you complete the Self Assessment Survey given later in this chapter. Viewed in total, the set of Plans provides the ingredients necessary for a successful marketing campaign built around e-mail newsletters.

Plan A. Use Your PC to Create, Launch and Manage a Text-Based E-Mail Newsletter.

Plan A is to use your own PC to prepare, send and manage a simple text-based e-mail newsletter on a regular basis. This is the easiest and lowest-cost way to have a newsletter. It also requires the lowest skill set to accomplish. Done right, however, text-based newsletters can have a positive impact by increasing your sales.

Skills Required: Basic PC and e-mail skills. Familiarity with Internet and navigating typical Websites.

Equipment Required: Any PC or Macintosh with an Internet connection and e-mail software.

Appropriate Number of Subscribers: A text-based newsletter may be used with any number of subscribers. However, list management quickly becomes burdensome beyond 50 subscribers.

Estimated Cost: $0 to $10 monthly, depending upon whether you utilize a Website in conjunction with your e-mail newsletter. Your agency or company may give you a free, directly-addressable Webpage (know as a "subdomain") for optional full-story content placement. If not, a Website can be created and operated for under $10 monthly if you feel you have the skills to do so.

Use in Conjunction with: Your agency or company Website – Try to get a linkable Webpage on this Website. This provides a location where your background can be presented and your listings can be referenced. Also use this page or another embedded Webpage (actually a subdomain such as *mystories.your agency.com*) to place the full content of linked articles included in your text-based e-mail newsletter.

References: See Chapters 4 and 9 for helpful information.

Plan B. Use Your PC with Free Internet Downloads to Create, Launch and Manage a Text-Based or Graphical E-Mail Newsletter.

Plan B is still PC-centric, but is the next step up in sophistication. It envisions supplementing your Microsoft-compatible PC and (Word and Outlook) Office software with compatible applications that can be downloaded free from Internet Websites. Some downloads are useful in managing text-based newsletters, but the preferred goal here is to create a graphically-oriented newsletter. The downloaded tools, such as HTML editors and list management, make it easier to design and manage colorful newsletters. They also enhance your productivity. If you are PC proficient and willing to learn new software, this is a cheap yet effective method to get your newsletter off the ground.

Skills Required: PC and Microsoft Office proficiency. Familiarity with the Internet and navigating typical Websites. Ability to download and learn new software.

Equipment Required: A PC or Macintosh with an Internet connection and Microsoft Word and Outlook software.

Appropriate Number of Subscribers: Determined by list management burden; likely to be impractical beyond 100 subscribers.

Use in Conjunction with: Your agency or company Website – Try to get a linkable Webpage on this Website. This provides a location where your background can be presented and your listings can be referenced. Also use this page or another embedded Webpage (actually a subdomain such as *mystories.your agency.com*) to place the full content of linked articles included in your e-mail newsletter.

Also consider launching your own Website (see Plan G) utilizing easy-to-understand tools provided by hosting vendors. Using your

<table>
<tr><td>

Estimated Cost: $0 to $10 monthly, depending upon whether your agency or company can give you a free, directly-addressable Webpage (know as a "subdomain").

</td><td>

newsletter to drive subscribers to a Website will significantly magnify the effectiveness of your marketing campaign.

References: See Chapters 4, 7 and 9 for helpful information.

</td></tr>
</table>

Plan C. Use Your PC with Commercial Software to Create, Launch and Manage a Graphical E-Mail Newsletter.

Again, Plan C is PC-centric, but yet another step up in sophistication. It envisions supplementing Microsoft Word and Outlook with compatible commercial software. These are fully integrated applications designed specifically to help you create, distribute and manage graphically-oriented newsletters. They include such tools as newsletter templates, HTML editors, automated list management functionality, perhaps some autoresponder capabilities and often a sales-oriented contact database. This software also makes it easier synchronize a newsletter campaign with activities and promotions highlighted on a Website.

The upfront cost is low and occurs only once. Anyone who has moderate PC skills can succeed with this plan.

Obviously, your productivity and effectiveness will be higher with an integrated approach to an e-mail marketing campaign. If you are PC proficient, not afraid to learn new software, and have the funds to acquire a commercial application, this is an effective means of quickly launching and easily managing your newsletter.

<table>
<tr><td>

Skills Required: PC and Microsoft Office proficiency. Familiarity with the Internet and navigating typical Websites. Must be willing to learn "drag and drop" HTML editing skills and how to use list management software. You also must be able to download or upload files to a Website using File Transfer Protocol (FTP) software (it's easy!).

Equipment Required: A late model PC with at least 10GB of available disk space, an Internet connection, and recent Microsoft operating (e.g., Windows XP or 2000) and Office software.

Appropriate Number of Subscribers: Determined by the list management burden, your PC bandwidth and the selected

</td><td>

Estimated One-Time Cost: $50 to $100 for newsletter preparation software, and $100 to $300 for an integrated list management application (depending on sophistication). Some good software is available that offers various degrees of both functionalities for about $100. Optionally, about $8 to $20 monthly for your own Website.

Use in Conjunction with: Your agency (or company) or your own Website.

If you do not have a personal Website for your business, it is strongly recommended that you utilize the hosting services of one of the vendors listed in Chapter 9 to create one (see Plan G). Using a newsletter to drive subscribers to your Website will significantly

</td></tr>
</table>

commercial software. A PC-centric approach, especially one where your PC is used as a "server" for outgoing e-mail and incoming message traffic, may become cumbersome beyond 150 – 200 subscribers and certainly difficult beyond 500 subscribers.

magnify your effectiveness and sales.

References: See Chapters 4, 8 and 9 for helpful information.

Plan D. Use Your PC to Create a Graphical E-Mail Newsletter, but Outsource its Distribution and Management.

If you have a large or fast-growing list of subscribers, this is the next step up in productivity. At some point, the effort required to sustain PC-centric approaches becomes overwhelming. When this happens, it is easier and better to have an outside vendor who has the equipment, sophisticated software and Internet bandwidth take over the burden of managing subscriptions and distributing your newsletter. This approach typically has the benefit of adding sophisticated autoresponders to your marketing arsenal as well.

While there is an ongoing cost involved, depending on your subscriber volume, it may not be significant. Many people have launched successful marketing campaigns by using commercial software on their desktop PC to create their graphical newsletter, then uploading it to an outsource vendor for distribution. And they have been able to do so while keeping their costs very low.

In fact, most vendors that provide list management services also offer online software to assist in the creation of HTML newsletters, so you don't even have to purchase this software for your desktop PC! Also, technical support for your list management is handled by the outsourcing vendor, relieving you of this headache if problems occur.

Thus, this is an excellent approach for even those new to e-mail newsletters. It is certainly easier than attempting to do everything on your own PC. Nonetheless, you are still responsible for creating the newsletter content.

Skills Required: PC and Microsoft Office proficiency. Familiarity with the Internet and navigating typical Websites. Must be willing to learn simple "drag and drop" HTML editing skills and how to use online list management software. You also must be able to download or upload files to a Website using File Transfer Protocol (FTP) software (it's easy!).

Estimated Ongoing Cost: Depends on the number of subscribers or e-mails distributed, but you can typically find a reputable service starting around $10 monthly. Optionally, add another $8 to $20 monthly to create your own Website.

Use in Conjunction with: Your agency (or company) Website or your own Website.

Equipment Required: A late model PC, an Internet connection, and recent Microsoft operating (e.g., Windows XP) is preferable.

Appropriate Number of Subscribers: Unlimited, since list management functions are handled at a Website hosted by the vendor maintaining these services.

If you do not have a personal Website for your business, it is strongly recommended that you utilize the hosting services of one of the vendors listed in Chapter 9 to create one (see Plan G). Using a newsletter to drive subscribers to your Website will significantly magnify your effectiveness and sales.

References: See Chapters 4, 8 and 10 for helpful information.

Plan E. Completely Outsource Your E-Mail Newsletter

If you do not have the time or skills to create and manage your own e-mail newsletter, then completely outsourcing this task is the way to go. Several online vendors exist who create newsletters for Realtors to send to their subscribers. These vendors also perform your list management functions, making this a relatively painless way to go.

The catch is, it's expensive compared to the other options and you give up flexibility in customizing the newsletter to your preferences. Your options are usually limited to having your photo and contact information included. However, you do get a professional-looking newsletter e-mailed monthly to your clientele. So, if spending several hundred dollars annually does not give you pause, then this may be the right approach for you.

Skills Required: Basic PC and e-mail skills. Familiarity with Internet and navigating typical Websites. Must be capable of uploading photo, contact information and subscriber list using vendor-provided online software.

Equipment Required: Any PC or Macintosh with an Internet connection and e-mail software.

Appropriate Number of Subscribers: Unlimited, since list management functions are handled at a Website hosted by the vendor maintaining these services.

Estimated Ongoing Cost: Minimum $300 annually. Optionally, add another $8 to $20 monthly to create your own Website.

Use in Conjunction with: Your agency (or company) Website or your own Website.

If you do not have a personal Website for your business, it is strongly recommended that you utilize the hosting services of one of the vendors listed in Chapter 9 to create one (see Plan G). Using a newsletter to drive subscribers to your Website will significantly magnify your effectiveness and sales.

References: See Chapters 4, 8 and 10 for helpful information.

Plan F. Supplement Plans A – E with a Dedicated Page on Your Company Website

Throughout this book, the benefits of having a Website have been emphasized. E-mail newsletters are a great way to drive your clients to your Website where you can present additional information and enhance your image as THE professional they should consider for current and future transactions. The success of any e-mail newsletter marketing campaign is greatly amplified if it is implemented in conjunction with a Website.

Having a Web presence can usually be accomplished with little or no cost by piggybacking on your agency or company Website (if one exists). Request your broker or president to provide a Webpage for your personal use. Often, this can be set up as a subdomain to allow you several Webpages for presenting and managing information. Here, you can present your "resume," lists (or links to listings) and the continued content o your newsletter. Sometimes, it is possible to handle list management functions on a subdomain as well.

Skills Required: Moderate PC and e-mail skills. Familiarity with Internet and typical Website layouts. Must be capable of using Web authoring tools (or have someone in the office who does this) and uploading information (using FTP tools).

Equipment Required: A late model PC with at least 10GB of available disk space, an Internet connection, and recent Microsoft operating (e.g., Windows XP or 2000) and Office software.

Appropriate Number of Subscribers: Unless your agency or company provides Web-based list management software, it will be necessary to continue to perform this function on your home-based PC, in which case you are likely to become overwhelmed after accumulating several hundred subscribers. Using an outside service for list management purposes circumvents this limitation.

Estimated Cost: $0 or whatever "rent" your office may charge.

Use in Conjunction with: Plans A – E. You will need access to your office Web authoring software or else purchase (or download free) software for your Desktop PC.

References: See Chapters 4, 8, 9 and 10 for helpful information.

Plan G. Supplement Plans A – E with Your Own Website

Another approach to having a Website is to create your own. This requires some confidence in your PC skills and a small monthly fee. However, the pay-off when used in partnership with an ongoing e-mail newsletter can be immense!

As stated earlier, you should not be deterred by a fear being technically incapable of creating a Website. Today, hosting vendors include a variety of easy-to-use tools and templates to assist you in this task. If you can use Microsoft Word at the level discussed in the first chapters, you can easily master the "drag and drop" functionality of Web authoring software or replace Webpage text in provided templates with your own.

Skills Required: Moderate PC and e-mail skills. Familiarity with Internet and typical Website layouts. Must be capable of using Web authoring tools (or have someone in the office who does this) and uploading information (using FTP tools).

Equipment Required: A late model PC with at least 10GB of available disk space, an Internet connection, and recent Microsoft operating (e.g., Windows XP or 2000) and Office software.

Appropriate Number of Subscribers:
Unless your agency or company provides Web-based list management software, it will be necessary to continue to perform this function on your home-based PC, in which case you are likely to become overwhelmed after accumulating several hundred subscribers. Using an outside service for list management purposes circumvents this limitation.

Estimated On-Going Cost: $10 or less monthly. Annual pre-paid contracts usually yield a 10 percent discount.

Use in Conjunction with: Plans A – E.

References: See Chapters 4, 8, 9 and 10 for helpful information.

Note that the emphasis throughout this book has been to present you with online resources and software solutions that are reputable yet don't cost "an arm and a leg." So whatever plan you decide on is not going to bankrupt you. The real questions you need to answer are related to your commitment and an honest assessment of your talents:

- How much time and effort do I really want to spend on launching a newsletter?

- Based on what I've read, what is my level of confidence in using Microsoft Word and Outlook, in being able to use host vendor tools to create a Website, or my ability to design a newsletter filled with interesting content?
- What are my expectations once I launch my newsletter? Do I understand that a newsletter is an ongoing project? Am I willing to give it time to work? Am I committed to making my newsletter successful?

You may find, for example, that the wisest course for you is to begin with a low-cost scenario and then upgrade your plan at a future date when you begin to see the returns form your efforts or have more financial resources. You may feel "This is simple. I can do this," and be ready to jump in feet first to accomplish everything on your PC. Or you may have concluded that while newsletters are certainly an effective marketing tool, the best course given your current situation is to simply outsource the whole thing. Whatever choice you make, be assured it will be the right one for you.

Rather than approaching a newsletter as a solo effort, also consider launching it as a group project that capitalizes on the time, resources and talents of your office colleagues. Maybe you feel comfortable about being able to create or gather newsletter content, but your PC skills are marginal. Is there a fellow Realtor or employee who has these talents? Why not join forces and both benefit from the results? If your finances or time is limited, approaching a periodic newsletter as a group project is an excellent way to share costs and share the work. Since each person in your agency has their own clients, an office newsletter is unlikely to be duplicated to the same prospects, so everyone benefits!

To help solidify your thinking and direct you to a suggested plan most likely to work for your unique situation, please begin by completing a short self-assessment to quantify your needs.

The First Step – A Self Assessment Survey

Assuming you have decided that an e-mail newsletter is a worthwhile activity, take a few moments to answer the questions below. This survey is intended to crystallize your thinking, resources and commitment. The more honest you are in your answers, the better the chances you will achieve an optimal plan of action which best fits your needs and capabilities.

Answer the following questions by indicating their "truth" of the statements as they fit your situation. Remember, the answer can reflect either a personal effort or a group activity. So decide before taking the quiz whether you intend to publish a newsletter alone or approach it with the help of others. "Yes" indicates agreement with the statement; "No" means you disagree with the statement as it pertains to you or your group.

Table 9. Self Assessment Survey

	Yes	No
1. I am prepared to perform activities necessary to procure and grow an opt-in list of e-mail addresses.	☐	☐
2. I have the time and commitment to spend 6-12 hours monthly on creating, publishing and managing an ongoing e-mail newsletter campaign.	☐	☐
3. Based on what I have learned in this book, I feel confident in my ability to create, publish and manage an e-mail newsletter campaign.	☐	☐
4. I have a PC or Macintosh with recent versions of Microsoft Word and Outlook (or someone in my group has a PC or Macintosh with this software).	☐	☐
5. My Microsoft Word and Outlook skills are at a level consistent with those necessary to create, publish and manage a newsletter using a desktop PC, or I feel confident in my (their) ability to learn these skills.	☐	☐
6. The one-time cost of acquiring PC software (Web authoring <u>and</u> list management software) is typically between $70 and $350. I can afford this expense.	☐	☐
The cost for outsourcing just the list management and distribution of a newsletter publication is generally $10 or less per month. I can afford this expense.	☐	☐
7. The cost for completely outsourcing the <u>preparation</u>, list management and distribution of a newsletter publication is a minimum $25 monthly or $350 annually. I can afford this expense.	☐	☐
8. My brokerage or company already has a Website, and I can get a personal page on this Website.	☐	☐
9. I have or intend to launch my own Website (under $10 monthly).	☐	☐

Before going further, write down your answers for each question. For example, "1. Y, 2. Y., etc." You will use this answer list in a moment to identify the best strategy for your circumstances.

Finding the Best Plan for You

Whether you answered "yes" or "no" to specific statements suggests one or more courses of action you should consider. But it is the composite of your choices that has real meaning. For it is only by considering all your answers that a realistic Plan (or set of Plans) can be formulated for your evaluation. Two tools are provided to assist you in this effort:

- The flow chart later in this chapter (Figure 5) provides an overview of the decision process. It demonstrates how your answers to each question indicate which plan (or plans) is (are) recommended for you. It also shows how the combination of your answers can lead to different conclusions.

  For example, gathering e-mail addresses is a basic prerequisite for conducting an e-mail newsletter campaign. So is having a PC or at least access to one. If these requirements cannot be satisfied, one should not even consider doing an email newsletter. Likewise, if you don't feel confident in being able to create an e-mail newsletter yourself, then your only choices are to outsource this process or else forego the newsletter.

  Take a moment to review the flow chart to gather an impression of the logic behind the selection process. But don't let yourself become bleary-eyed by looking at it, because....

- It is followed a chart on the next page (Figure 6.) where <u>all you have to do is find the row that contains a copy of your Self Assessment answers to see the recommended Plans that best fit your situation.</u> For example, if your answers to the Self Assessment questions were:

Questions:	1	2	3	4	5	6	7	8	9	10
Answers:	Y	Y	Y	Y	Y	N	N	N	Y	N

This matches the answer profile found in row 10. Looking to the right, you can see that the practical course of action for you to consider is Plan B (use your own PC with free downloads) supplemented by Plan F (seek a Webpage on your agency or company Website). This makes sense. You're willing to do the work, have a PC, and are confident in your skills, but you're strapped for funds. So, take advantage of your talents and use freebies off the Web to create and manage a newsletter. And, see if you can get free space on your agency or company Website to promote yourself and store your newsletter content.

Find the row of Survey answers that matches yours. Highlight this row for future reference. This is your unique starting plan. As conditions change, your answers to the Survey may change and you can easily update your plan.

Formulating Your Action Plan

Once you have settled on a plan of action, return to the referenced chapters to select the best answer for you from among the listed desktop software applications, free Web downloads, Website hosting vendors or outsource vendors.

Summarize Your Strategy

Use the form found in Table 9 to summarize your strategy. Enter your choices and summarize the costs, if any, that you can expect to incur. Step back and ask yourself, "Is this the strategy I want to pursue? Is it a good match for my talents, time restrictions and resources? If I do this, will it satisfy my goals?" If your answers are "yes" to all these questions, then you are ready to proceed. If not, then review your answers to the Self Assessment Survey to pinpoint where the conflict exists.

Prepare an Action Plan

Begin by drawing up an action plan. Lay out the steps you need to follow to successfully launch your newsletter. What will you do first? What is the next step after that? Continue this process until you have a cohesive plan of action leading to your ultimate goal.

The major steps in your action plan should include:

1. Using the charts and tables in this book, investigate the software and/or outsource service options indicated by my Plan(s). Pick one of each (reference Chapters 7, 8 and 9 as appropriate).

2. *Finalize My Strategy* using the summary chart provided later in this chapter. This tells you how you will create your newsletter, where you will get content, and how you intend to distribute and manage it.

3. Develop your newsletter layout using your PC, possibly supplemented by tools obtained by purchasing commercial software or outside services (reference Chapters 7, 8 and 9 as necessary).

4. Create your newsletter content (reference Chapter 5).

5. Meanwhile, implement a process to collect opt-in e-mail addresses from customers and prospective clients (reference Chapter 6).

6. If Website development is part of your plan, begin work on this (reference Chapter 10).

7. Implement a manual or automated process to manage your mail list, handling at minimum new subscribers, "unsubscribes" and bounced e-mail (reference Chapters 6, 7, 8 and 9 as appropriate).

8. When everything is ready, begin your newsletter distribution.

9. Set up an ongoing process to create content for a monthly or quarterly newsletter distribution.

10. Perform ongoing management of your newsletter marketing campaign.

11. Track your newsletter results (# e-mail openings, Website visits generated by the newsletter, etc.) to measure its effectiveness (reference Chapters 7, 8, 9 and 10 as appropriate); fine-tune your newsletter content and layout as necessary. If you have a Website (or Webpage on your company or agency Website), fine-tune its material and navigation if necessary to enhance attractiveness, subscriber recruitment and ease of use. Also track new revenues that can be directly related to your newsletter to measure your return on investment.

Figure 5. Survey Logic

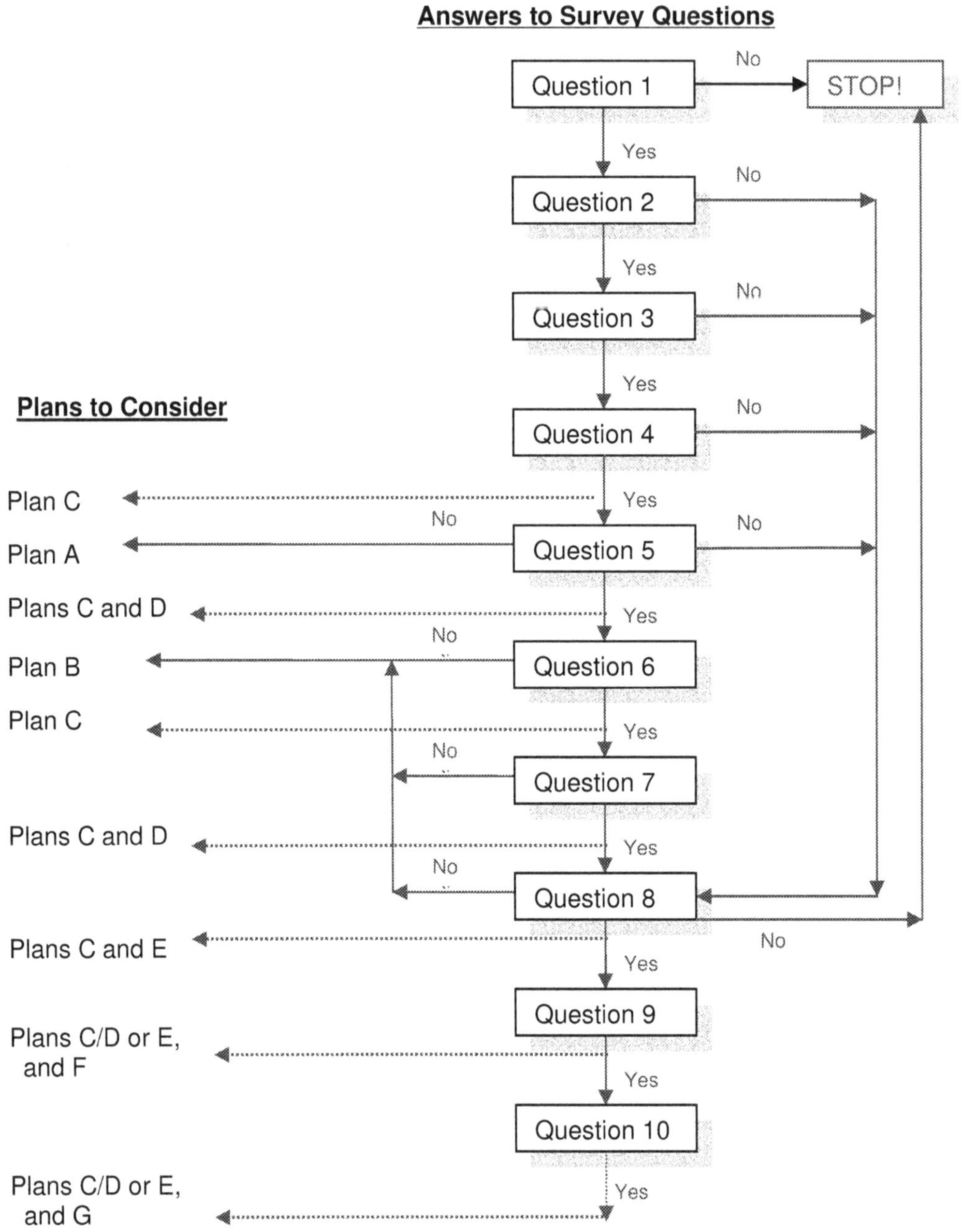
Answers to Survey Questions
Plans to Consider
Question 1
Question 2
Question 3
Question 4
Question 5
Question 6
Question 7
Question 8
Question 9
Question 10
STOP!
Yes
No
Plan C
Plan A
Plans C and D
Plan B
Plan C
Plans C and D
Plans C and E
Plans C/D or E, and F
Plans C/D or E, and G

Figure 6. Translating Survey Answers into Plans of Action

Then the Plans to consider are:

- Plan A. Use PC for Text-Based Newsletter
- Plan B. Use PC with free downloads
- Plan C. Use PC with commercial software
- Plan D. Outsource list mgmt & distribution
- Plan E. Completely outsource
- Plan F. Separate page on company Website
- Plan G. Establish own Website

If your answers to the Survey are:

Row	1	2	3	4	5	6	7	8	9	10	A	B	C	D	E	F	G
1	N	Any Answer									Forget about doing an e-mail newsletter						
2	Y	N	Any Answer					N	Any		Forget about doing an e-mail newsletter						
3	Y	Y	N	Any Answer				N	Any		Forget about doing an e-mail newsletter						
4	Y	Y	Y	N	Any Answer			N	Any		Forget about doing an e-mail newsletter						
5	Y	Y	N	Any Answer				Y	Any						X		
6	Y	Y	Y	Y	N	Any		N	Any		X						
7	Y	Y	Y	Y	N	Any		Y	Any		X				X		
8	Y	Y	Y	Y	N	N	N	N	Y	N	X					X	
9	Y	Y	Y	Y	Y	N	N	N	N	N		X					
10	Y	Y	Y	Y	Y	N	N	N	Y	N		X				X	
11	Y	Y	Y	Y	Y	N	N	N	N	Y		X					X
12	Y	Y	Y	Y	Y	N	N	N	Y	Y		X				X	X
13	Y	Y	Y	Y	Y	N	Y	N	N	N		X		X			
14	Y	Y	Y	Y	Y	N	Y	N	Y	N		X		X		X	
15	Y	Y	Y	Y	Y	N	Y	N	N	Y		X		X			X
16	Y	Y	Y	Y	Y	N	Y	N	Y	Y		X		X		X	X
17	Y	Y	Y	Y	Y	N	Y	Y	Y	Y		X		X	X	X	X
18	Y	Y	Y	Y	Y	Y	N	N	N	N			X				
19	Y	Y	Y	Y	Y	Y	N	N	Y	N			X			X	
20	Y	Y	Y	Y	Y	Y	N	N	N	Y			X				X
21	Y	Y	Y	Y	Y	Y	N	N	Y	Y			X			X	X
22	Y	Y	Y	Y	Y	Y	Y	Y	N	N			X	X	X		
23	Y	Y	Y	Y	Y	Y	Y	Y	Y	N			X		X	X	
24	Y	Y	Y	Y	Y	Y	Y	Y	N	Y			X	X	X		X
25	Y	Y	Y	Y	Y	Y	Y	Y	Y	Y			X	X	X	X	X

Table 10. My Strategy

1. **The Plans comprising my strategy are (check all that apply):**

Plan A. I will use my PC to create, launch and manage a text-based e-mail newsletter. ☐

Plan B. I will use my PC with free Internet downloads to create, launch and manage either a text-based ☐ or graphical ☐ e-mail newsletter, or both ☐.

Plan C. I will use my PC with commercial software to create, launch and manage a graphical e-mail newsletter. ☐

Plan D. I will use my PC to create a graphical e-mail newsletter, but outsource its distribution and management. ☐

Plan E. I will completely outsource my e-mail newsletter. ☐

Plan F. I will supplement my above choice(s) with a dedicated page on my agency or company Website. ☐

Plan G. I will supplement my above choice(s) with my own Website. ☐

2. **Free software (if any) that I will download from Internet Web sites is:**

List Management (Software or Service): _____

Microsoft Outlook Plug-Ins: _____

HTML Editor: _____

Other: _____

3. **Commercial software (if any) I will purchase for my desktop PC is:**

Newsletter Preparation: _____ Cost: _____

Web Authoring (for HTML newsletter or Website creation): _____

_____ Cost: _____

List Management: _____ Cost: _____

Other: _____ Cost: _____

4. Outside services (if any) I intend to use are:

Complete Newsletter Process (preparation, distribution and list management):

_____ Cost: _____

List Management: _____ Cost: _____

Website Hosting Vendor: _____ Cost: _____

Newsletter Content: _____ Cost: _____

Other: _____ Cost:_____

5. I will get my newsletter content from:

An outside service (see above). ☐   Create it myself. ☐   Use or modify free sources. ☐

The free sources I will review are: _____

_____

_____

6. I will create and manage a newsletter:

By myself. ☐   Working with a group of associates. ☐

12. THE BOTTOM LINE

Like everything else in real estate, creating and managing e-mail newsletters takes work. Even when everything is outsourced, you still have to collect e-mail addresses and have a method for attracting new subscribers. To accomplish marketing campaigns based on e-mail newsletters, you must be prepared to a commitment to not only the effort involved, but also the time and money necessary to make your newsletter successful.

If you are committed to making your newsletter successful, and you have a PC and some basic skills, then deciding on the best course of action is just a matter of how much time you have and how much money you are willing to spend.

To a great extent, the cost of conducting an e-mail newsletter campaign is determined by the number of subscribers involved. For those just launching a newsletter, a typical progression might be:

- You choose to begin your newsletter with minimal cost, doing everything on a desktop PC with free downloads off the Web.

- At a certain point, the volume hits a threshold where it becomes unwieldy or too time consuming to manage your subscriber list (adding and removing subscribers, sending confirmations, handling bounced e-mails, etc.) with your limited software.

- At that time, perhaps commercial PC software is purchased to alleviate the situation.

- But even this solution has its limitations. So, as your number of subscribers grows, list management operations are moved to an outsource vendor utilizing sophisticated applications in conjunction with more powerful Web server equipment and a larger Internet bandwidth.

Thus, as subscriber volume increases over time, you can expect to upgrade your resources and methodologies. The expense involved roughly correlates with Plans A through G, which demonstrates a natural progression in sophistication and productivity.

Figure 7. Expense Generally Increases as Subscriber Volume Increases

Plans E & G	($30+ monthly)	
Plans C, D & G	(As low as $100 one-time cost, but typically $150-$400; $20+ monthly for own Website and using outsource list mgmt)	
Plans C & D	(As low as $100 one-time cost, but typically $150-$400; $10+ monthly for using outsource list mgmt)	
Plan C or Plans C & F	(As low as $100 one-time cost, but typically $150-$400; may be rental charge for using company Website)	
Plans A & B	($0-$10 Monthly)	

Expense ($)

Subscribers

Regardless of the strategy employed, you can see that the cost involved in publishing and managing a monthly or quarterly newsletter is not horrendous. In fact, you can probably create a graphical newsletter on your PC using commercial software designed for this purpose, outsource your list management and have your own Website for just $100 upfront cost and less than $20 monthly. This is a small price to pay for the potential returns you can expect.

The two keys to being successful with a newsletter campaign are to be consistent and to continually grow your subscription list. Once you begin a newsletter, be it monthly or quarterly, commit yourself to publishing it according to a regular schedule. Your newsletter is just another (albeit powerful) arrow in your marketing quiver. And in real estate, nothing works better than consistency, or as we say "Drip, drip, drip information to maintain awareness among your clients."

Once launched, especially if you implant a marketing campaign integrated with your Website, your newsletter will take on a momentum of its own. But you must always nurture processes which contribute to growing your subscription base. After all, sales is a numbers game, and the more people reading your newsletter, the more revenue you can expect to generate as a result of your efforts.

Be sure to enter this endeavor with the right expectations. It takes time to create and properly launch a newsletter. Once you begin, it can take even more time to see tangible results. Nonetheless, you immediately begin to benefit from intangible results, such as increased awareness among potential customers, forwarding of your newsletter to friends, co-workers and relatives, worldwide exposure from your website, etc. Sooner or later, these factors will result in new business for you. Widespread use of e-mail newsletters in Corporate America has proven that they work. And, when you visit Websites selling newsletter services, you will see excited endorsements by Realtors extolling their effectiveness in generating new leads that have doubled or tripled their business. So recognize upfront that it takes a while for a newsletter to pick up momentum. Be patient and just keep plugging away. Depending on your situation, you can expect to see new leads in as little as 30 to 60 days of your initial launch. It may take longer, but don't give up! Sooner or later, the small ongoing effort you put into a periodic newsletter will translate into money in your pocket.

Having digested the material in this book, you are a giant step ahead of your competition. Use that advantage to increase your local market share. Newsletters "push" your message into the homes and businesses of the people you want to employ your services. It is a trade-off: you give them valuable information in exchange for access. As long as this equation remains balanced, your subscriber list will grow and a revenue upswing will surely follow.

Successful Realtors and services addressing the real estate industry are entrepreneurs. You live by your wits and essentially run your own business. Your eye is always on the bottom line. Your time is precious. That is why you need a marketing tool that fits your pocketbook and works twenty-four hours a day for you. E-mail newsletters, especially when combined with a personal Website, are one of today's most effective means of holding onto existing clients while generating new ones. The ultimate rewards more than justify the time and resources poured into creating and managing this effective marketing tool.

You now have the knowledge. You have the means. You have the commitment. Go make it happen.

Good luck!

Appendix 1 – Low-Priced Newsletter and

Web Authoring Software for Your Desktop PC

Item	Description
Product Name	Easy Web Editor
Vendor	VisualVision
Website	http://www.easywebeditor.com
Overview *(Based on verbiage from vendor Website)*	Thanks to its hypertext orientated environment, you can even build complicated sites without having to be on-line for a single minute. Multiple hyperlinked pages are simultaneously available for editing, and you can visually place any kind of link, including the ones pointing to separate windows or frames. You can browse pages without exiting the editor, you can search and replace words globally, and define keywords... all with a few clicks. The visual editor supports tables, maps, frame sets, slides, forms, windows opening, mouse-over changing images, style-sheets and much more - all in WYSIWYG. When your pages are finished, you can publish them to the Internet with a single click. The internal FTP engine optimizes the upload by recognizing modified pages; the resulting HTML (automatically generated) is compatible with any browser. In short, no overly technical stuff; you can concentrate purely on content and on site design, leaving Easy Web Editor to automatically take care of the rest. This is a good, low-priced choice for novices to create HTML-based newsletters and Websites.
System Requirements	For Windows 95, 98, Me, NT, 2000, XP, 2003.
Price	**$59.95 for single-user license (when downloaded)**
Special Offers	FREE trial can be downloaded to decide if you want to purchase the software.
Upgrades	Complementary software is available on Website for ordering.

Appendix 1: Low-Priced Newsletter and Web Authoring Software for Your Desktop PC

Item	Description
Product Name	High Impact eMail 2.0
Vendor	Template Zone
Website	www.templatezone.com
Overview *(Based on verbiage from vendor Website)*	High Impact eMail 2.0 is an innovative add-on for Microsoft Outlook, Outlook Express, and ACT! that makes it possible for any Outlook user to send graphical HTML emails, newsletters and advertisements in just minutes. High Impact eMail can take your email to a higher level - look more professional with branded email stationery; launch successful email marketing campaigns; start sending a monthly or quarterly email newsletter to your subscribers, clients and prospects. High Impact eMail is the perfect low-cost tool for the small business user who wants to leverage the amazing power of email. Offers free 250KB of web space for online image storage. Includes 400 templates.
System Requirements	Windows 95 (minimal), Windows 98, Windows ME, Windows NT 4, Windows 2000, Windows XP Home & Pro Edition. Compatible with Outlook 98, Outlook 2000, Outlook XP or Outlook Express 5, ACT! 6.0 and higher.
Price	**$49.95 for single-user license** **2MB of online image storage: $19.95 for one year; $39.95 for two years.** **5MB of online image storage: $39.95 for one year; $59.95 for two years.**
Special Offers	FREE Newsletter Template Pack-Volume 1
Upgrades	Add more templates.

Appendix 1: Low-Priced Newsletter and Web Authoring Software for Your Desktop PC

Item	Description
Product Names	Publisher 2003
Vendor	Microsoft
Website	http://www.amazon.com
Overview *(Based on verbiage from vendor Website)*	Office Publisher 2003 is the Microsoft Office business publishing and marketing materials program. Keeping in touch and communicating with customers is essential for any business – you can use Publisher 2003 to help you create professional marketing materials in-house, quickly and efficiently. Create a comprehensive selection of business publications using new wizards, such as the Easy Web Site Builder and the E-Mail Newsletter wizard. Automatically create a publication that merges pictures and text from a data source (like Microsoft Excel or Microsoft Access) using Catalog Merge to create publications ranging from a datasheet to a sophisticated catalog. This is a top of the line choice for novices to create e-mail newsletters, Website materials or just about any type of marketing or sales aid.
System Requirements	Microsoft Windows 2000, Microsoft Windows 98, Microsoft Windows ME, Microsoft Windows XP; requires 250MB disk storage.
Price	**$120-150 for single-user license**
Special Offers	FREE trial can be downloaded to decide if you want to purchase the software.
Upgrades	Complementary software is available on Website for ordering.

Appendix 1: Low-Priced Newsletter and Web Authoring Software for Your Desktop PC

Item	Description
Product Name	SiteSpinner v2
Vendor	Virtual Mechanics
Website	http://www.virtualmechanics.com/index.html
Overview *(Based on verbiage from vendor Website)*	**You don't need to know any HTML** - SiteSpinner V2 is 100% WYSIWYG - move anything anywhere with your mouse. **No need for image editing software** - Change the size or properties of any picture right in the work-window. **No need for a paint program** - Create shapes, backgrounds. Add shading or transparency. **No need for FTP software** - Publish directly from SiteSpinner V2 to your web host. All your images can be automatically uploaded too. This is a polished, feature-rich solution for creating Websites. More than you need for just a newsletter, but recommended if you're thinking about (or already have) a Website.
System Requirements	For Windows 95, 98, Me, NT, 2000, XP, 2003.
Price	**$49 for single-user license (when downloaded)**
Special Offers	FREE trial can be downloaded to decide if you want to purchase the software.
Upgrades	Complementary software is available on Website for ordering.

Appendix 1: Low-Priced Newsletter and Web Authoring Software for Your Desktop PC

Item	Description
Product Names	Web Author with Image Mapper
Vendor	101ware.com
Website	http://www.101ware.com/splash/
Overview *(Based on verbiage from vendor Website)*	Splash! Web Author has practically no learning curve for even the newest Internet user because of its 'no-code' environment. It allows you the power to utilize even the most powerful of web based publishing languages without having to learn a line of code. Splash! Web Author isn't a simple fill in the blanks template editor, its drag-and-drop WYSIWYG interface allows you full control over where your pictures and text will appear on your page and how they will look. Splash! ImageMapper is included within the Web Author program. The image mapper allows you to set boundaries within an image and place links in each area. An online tutorial is available. This is a good, low-priced choice for beginners to create HTML-based newsletters and simple Websites.
System Requirements	Windows-based PC.
Price	**$19.95 for single-user license of Web Authoring (when downloaded)**
Special Offers	FREE 21-day demo can be downloaded to decide if you want to purchase the software.
Upgrades	None

Appendix 1: Low-Priced Newsletter and Web Authoring Software for Your Desktop PC

Item	Description
Product Name	Webpage Creation Kit
Vendor	Boomerang Software
Website	http://www.boomerangsoftware.com
Overview *(Based on verbiage from vendor Website)*	A complete toolbox for creating Web pages that give your site the look and feel you want. Get started quickly by using professionally designed templates and wizards, create and edit your own site graphics, add navigation bars, and generate HTML tables and frames. Easy to use, it features all the sophistication you want. This is an excellent choice to create e-mail newsletters and Websites. More than you need for just a newsletter, but recommended if you're thinking about (or already have) a Website.
System Requirements	Operating system: Microsoft Windows 98/Me/NT 4.0/2000/XP Processor: 100 MHz Pentium or better (recommended) Memory: 64 MB RAM (recommended) Free Hard Drive Space: 100 MB (recommended) Monitor: VGA or higher resolution monitor with 256 colors Peripherals: CD-ROM, mouse, and keyboard
Price	**$59.95 for single-user license**
Special Offers	FREE 30-day trial can be downloaded to decide if you want to purchase the software.
Upgrades	Complementary software is available.

Item	Description
Product Name	WebEasy
Vendor	VCOM
Website	www.v-com.com
Overview *(Based on verbiage from vendor Website)*	‣ Designed with the first time Web developer in mind, Web Easy also offers the flexibility to please even the more sophisticated user. ‣ Access to VCOM's 50,000+ library of clipart, photos, animated graphics, backgrounds, buttons, frames, and more for inclusion In Web Easy's dynamic pages from CD and on-line. (30,000+ included on CD) ‣ Over 50 professional multi-page templates ‣ Free trial Hosting This is a good choice to create e-mail newsletters and Websites. More than you need for just a newsletter, but recommended if you're thinking about (or already have) a Website.
System Requirements	Windows 98/Me/2000/XP Pentium or better 32 MB RAM 150 MB free hard disk space CD Drive, Mouse 800 x 600, 16-bit color display or better Internet access required for posting your completed web site and accessing VCOM's online Library
Price	**$39.95 for single-user license**
Special Offers	None
Upgrades	Complementary software and Website hosting is available.

Item	Description
Product Name	WebEditor6
Vendor	SJ Namo
Website	http://www.boomerangsoftware.com
Overview *(Based on verbiage from vendor Website)*	• WebEditor 6 Suite is an all-in-one tool you need to easily create and manage <u>Personal</u> and <u>Professional</u> Web sites. Beginners and advanced users alike will appreciate WebEditor's design and script templates, site resource management features, <u>Integrated</u> graphics features, and more. • In addition to having WebCanvas 1.1, the vector-based Web graphic drawing tool, WebEditor 6 Suite now features WebBoard 1.1, a Web community builder tool which will set up any number of forums through a simple <u>Windows</u> <u>Application</u> on your <u>Desktop</u> This is an excellent choice to create e-mail newsletters and Websites. More than you need for just a newsletter, but recommended if you're thinking about (or already have) a Website.
System Requirements	Microsoft Windows 98/Me/NT/2000/XP; Microsoft <u>Internet</u> Explorer 4.0 or newer, Netscape 6.2 or newer, 800x600 (1,024x768 recommended), 256-color display or better recommended, 64 MB of <u>RAM</u> (128 MB of RAM or higher recommended), Microsoft Personal Web <u>Server</u> or Internet Information Server required for preview of database-driven documents, Hard <u>Disk</u> space: Namo WebEditor - 48 MB.
Price	**$69.99 for single-user license (after rebate)**
Special Offers	None
Upgrades	Complementary software is available.

Item	Description
Product Name	WebExpress
Vendor	MicroVision
Website	http://www.mvd.com/webexpress/
Overview (Based on verbiage from vendor Website)	WebExpress gets you started with dozens of customizable templates, so you can create professional looking Web sites and be up on the Web instantly. This software tool walks you through the complete creation process with many helpful Wizards, templates and a gallery of graphics. It supports all the latest Web bells and whistles including multimedia, sound, video and more. Plus, capture valuable visitor information with interactive forms. This is a good choice to create e-mail newsletters and Websites. More than you need for just a newsletter, but recommended if you're thinking about (or already have) a Website.
System Requirements	Microsoft Windows 98/Me/NT/2000/XP
Price	**$69.95 for single-user license**
Special Offers	FREE trial copy.
Upgrades	Complementary software is available.

Item	Description
Product Name	Web Studio 4.0
Vendor	Back To The Beach Software
Website	http://www.webstudio.com
Overview *(Based on verbiage from vendor Website)*	With Web Studio, **what you see is what you get**, just like in your favorite graphics and desktop publishing software. **No HTML programming** is required! **Wizards and templates** guide you from page layout to photo manipulation to uploading your site. Our new "trial publishing" feature, lets you **preview any page - or your entire site - live on the web**. This is an excellent choice to create e-mail newsletters and Websites. More than you need for just a newsletter, but recommended if you're thinking about (or already have) a Website.
System Requirements	Microsoft Windows 2000, Microsoft Windows 98, Microsoft Windows ME, Microsoft Windows XP; requires 250MB disk storage.
Price	**$89.99 for single-user license (when downloaded)**
Special Offers	FREE 30-day trial can be downloaded to decide if you want to purchase the software.
Upgrades	Complementary software is available.

Appendix 2 – Low-Priced E-Mail Newsletter

List Management Software for Your Desktop PC

Appendix 2 – Low-Priced E-Mail Newsletter List Management Software for Your PC

Item	Description
Vendor	WriteExpress
Website	http://www.writeexpress.com/hi/high-impact-email.htm
Product Name	High Impact E-Mail
Overview *(Based on verbiage from vendor Website)*	*High Impact eMail* has 400+ HTML email templates for creating newsletters, ads, forms, price lists, greeting cards, stationery and more. Simply edit with your own text and images. The profile feature automatically inserts contact information, your logo, portrait and signature to easily and quickly personalize an email. In minutes, you're ready to dazzle your customers, prospects and colleagues with rich, colorful HTML email. Great-looking HTML templates come with preformatted designs and image placeholders. The templates also make it easy for you to insert your message text. Now you can send out email advertisements, notify customers of upcoming sales or specials - and look like a pro doing it. ReadyShare, a **FREE** service (250KB) included with *High Impact eMail* version 2.0, lets you upload images to the web and then include those images in your HTML email. Now you can send email with product photos or images that highlight and enhance the words in the message. Email will get noticed and sales will increase. This may be a good choice for those without a Website who are just getting started.
System Requirements	**Office Suite:** Microsoft Office 2000 or XP **Platform:** Windows® XP, 2000, 98, 95, NT, or Me **CPU:** Pentium® 300 MHz or faster **RAM:** 32 MB (64 MB recommended) **Disk Space:** 40 MB available disk space **Display:** 640x480 Display, 16-bit color or better **Browser:** Netscape 4.02 and higher, Internet Explorer 4.x and higher (Internet Explorer 5.X, Internet Explorer 6.X, or higher recommended) **Application compatibility** Outlook 98, Outlook 2000, Outlook XP or Outlook Express 5, ACT! 6.0 and higher
Price	**$79.95 for CD; $49.95 when downloaded (11.2MB)**
Special Offers	Includes **FREE** Newsletter Template Pack Vol I (15 HTML templates) and **FREE** Newsletter eMarketing eBook when downloaded.
Upgrades	Additional ReadyShare storage can be rented. Newsletter Template Pack Vol II - Offers 2, 4, and 6 page designs that work with Microsoft Word: $29.95.

Appendix 2 – Low-Priced E-Mail Newsletter List Management Software for Your PC

Item	Description
Vendor	Act!
Website	http://www.act.com/
Product Name	Act! 6.0 for 2004
Overview *(Based on verbiage from vendor Website)*	Claimed to be the #1 best-selling contact management solution — used by millions. When ordered in North America, ACT! now includes synchronization software for Palm OS and Pocket PC handhelds. Trans/ACT! Residential is a complete system for marketing your services to home owners and buyers (http://www.act.com/realestate). Act! is a widely-used by sales people and is fully compatible – and interfaces - with Microsoft Outlook. Although primarily focused on contact management, it also includes the ability to send HTML e-mails and includes 10 modifiable newsletter templates. If you want a powerful package that tracks client interaction and your sales pipeline while also supporting graphical newsletters, Act! is a good choice: • Manage all your customer information in one place. • Stay on top of your schedule with ease. • Create and send personalized letters, faxes, and e-mails . • Meet your sales goals with confidence. • Share complete customer information in a workgroup environment. • Works with Microsoft Outlook, handheld devices, paper organizers, and other popular products. The major shortcomings are a lack of e-mail list management and subscribe/unsubscribe functionality. Nonetheless, <u>this may be a good choice if you already have access to a Website with these capabilities.</u>
System Requirements	• Microsoft Windows® 98/Me/NT/2000/XP operating system. • Minimum 60 MB of free hard disk space. • CD-ROM drive. • 133 MHz processor or higher. • 64 MB of memory or higher. • VGA or higher monitor resolution. • Microsoft Internet Explorer® 5.5/6.0. • Windows-compatible modem required for auto-dialing or modem-based synchronization.
Price	**$229.95 when downloaded**
Special Offers	When ordered in North America, ACT! now includes synchronization software for Palm OS and Pocket PC handhelds and ACT! for Palm OS for a limited time ($79.95 value). For a limited time, a download version of High Impact eMail for ACT! (over 400 HTML email templates) will also be included FREE with a purchase of ACT! 6.0 for 2004!

Appendix 2 – Low-Priced E-Mail Newsletter List Management Software for Your PC

Item	Description
Vendor	BlueLark
Website	http://www.bluelark.com/
Product Name	NewsletterPro
Overview *(Based on verbiage from vendor Website)*	NewsletterPro offers an e-mail newsletter system that allows you to easily keep in touch with your customers, and requires no technical knowledge of HTML or customer database setup. It includes everything that you need to run your email marketing campaigns - a list builder, subscription forms, newsletter editor, tracking, reports and more! Completely Web-based, you do not need to download or install any additional software on your PC. Everything runs directly from your web browser, meaning that you have 24/7 access to NewsletterPro from any computer with a browser and an internet connection. This might be a good solution if you or your company already has a Website with the requisite software features necessary to support NewsletterPro.
System Requirements	Web server with: UNIX/Linux/FreeBSD/Solaris/Windows Apache, IIS or any web server that supports PHP PHP 4.1.0 or higher MySQL 3.23 or higher Web Client (Browser) IE 5.0 or higher
Price	**$99 per Website; includes free installation and technical support.**
Special Offers	Free lifetime upgrades as they become available.

Appendix 2 – Low-Priced E-Mail Newsletter List Management Software for Your PC

Item	Description
Vendor	Sprika Software
Website	http://www.sprika.com/litemail.htm
Product Name	Lite Mail 2.2
Overview *(Based on verbiage from vendor Website)*	LiteMail 2.2 supports attachments, HTML, Image Embedding, Internal SMTP Server, subscriptions, multipart messages, several list management features and more. You can import existing email mailing lists from comma-separated files, Windows Address Book, as well as Access databases (.mdb). List management functions include sorting, cleaning and search. You can send the bulk email messages, using your ISPs SMTP server - LiteMail supports authentication, in case your ISP requires it. Also, an inbuilt SMTP server is now added. LiteMail automatically embeds images in all outgoing HTML messages. You can send multipart messages (both text and HTML in the same message) for recipients who use older email clients. The program also supports basic e-mail merging, allowing you to customize the email message with the current date, the recipients e-mail, and more. LiteMail can also process incoming email messages (Subscribes and Un-subscribes). If you have a little technical savvy, this could be a good desktop solution to handle some basic functions (e.g., subscribe/unsubscribe). Consider also purchasing eVerify (see below) to handle bounced e-mails. Not recommended for beginners.
System Requirements	Pentium 200 MHZ 32 MB RAM 25 MB Hard Disk Windows 98/ME/2000/XP
Price	**$20 for single-user license.**
Special Offers	For a limited time, get the full version of LiteMail 2.2 for free when you purchase eVerify (handles bounced e-mails), *a $20 Value.*

Appendix 2 – Low-Priced E-Mail Newsletter List Management Software for Your PC

Item	Description
Vendor	AdComplete.com
Website	http://www.enewsletterpro.com/
Product Name	eNewsletter Pro
Overview *(Based on verbiage from vendor Website)*	eNewsletter Pro is email newsletter software for managing and distributing HTML or Text formatted newsletters via email. The product supports an unlimited number of mailing lists and newsletters. Each person can subscribe to one or more Newsletter Lists. The system uses a confirmed opt-in method to prevent malicious behavior. Good solution if you have a Microsoft server handling your Website. Does not include HTML editor (unless you buy the Enterprise version for $389) or templates.
System Requirements	eNewsletter Pro was developed exclusively for web sites hosted on Windows NT/Windows 2000 **Servers.**
Price	**$369 for single-user license.**
Special Offers	None

Item	Description
Vendor	EXP Elite, Inc.
Website	http://www.extractorpro.com/
Product Name	Elite
Overview *(Based on verbiage from vendor Website)*	EXP Elite is a top of the line opt-in Internet marketing & email contact management desktop software tool. Major benefits are: • It sends out opt-in e-mail to your subscribers for you - 24 hours a day, 7 days a week. • Checks your email before you send it to make sure it's not mistakenly tagged as spam • Works as your own personal newsletter server - stop paying high monthly fees for this service. • Sends both Text & HTML messages - EXP Elite knows which your subscriber can read. • Built-in customer database manager. • Contains a smart "Sequential" Autoresponder solution - with both unlimited accounts and follow ups. • Tracks the success / fail ratio of your outgoing email campaigns so you'll know exactly how much of your mail was delivered! Good desktop solution if you can afford it. Doesn't include HTML editor or templates, but these can be found free elsewhere on the Web.
System Requirements	EXP elite was built using the most current Microsoft drivers and access database. It was designed specifically for Windows XP, ME, and 98.
Price	**$229 for single-user license.**
Special Offers	Includes FREE "SMTP Phantom" to erase the limitations set by your ISP! ($99 value) and EXP Elite's Spam Filter Checker.

Appendix 2 – Low-Priced E-Mail Newsletter List Management Software for Your PC

Item	Description
Vendor	4OfficeAutomation
Website	http://www.4officeautomation.com/EmailUnlimited/index.asp
Product Name	EmailUnlimited 6.0
Overview *(Based on verbiage from vendor Website)*	EmailUnlimited makes it easy to send professional-looking email messages to large lists of recipients: *Just select your address list, type in your message or select an existing text or HTML file, click on the send button and your customers will soon be informed about your newest products and offerings.* *Email Unlimited has a low learning curve and ease-of-use for your convenience.* They have added on-screen instructions and an intuitive user interface, which will help you to configure EmailUnlimited faster than any other desktop-based email marketing solution. EmailUnlimited 6.0 Standard provides all necessary for sending mailings, processing auto-responses and maintaining your email list, such as: <ul><li>Full HTML Capability</li><li>Preview Mode</li><li>Automated Mailing List Maintenance (subscribe/unsubscribe/NDR processing)</li><li>Form Handler</li><li>Follow-up Auto Responders</li><li>Scheduled Mailings</li><li>Recent Mailing Manager</li><li>Supported formats: Access, Excel, CSV, dBase, Works and Outlook Contact Lists</li></ul>A good package for those who are Outlook savvy and committed to having a desktop solution. Oriented towards list and mail management. Auto responder is a plus. Let's you schedule customized e-mail sales letters too. Lacks some HTML features - does not include newsletter templates. Some functions require manual intervention, but this is definitely a productivity tool. EmailUnlimited circumvents ISP spam issues by automatically disconnecting and reconnecting after 10 messages, and thus works around ISP e-mail broadcast limitations.
System Requirements	EmailUnlimited will run on any computer running Windows 95 and Microsoft Internet Explorer 4.0 or higher. Of course, it will also run on computers with Windows 98, Windows Me, Windows 2000 Professional, Windows XP, Windows NT 4.0 Sp3 (meaning Service Pack 3 is required) Client and Server Edition.
Price	**$197 for single-user license.**
Special Offers	Lease for $19.95 monthly (includes free updates). They also offer a Web services supplement for $14.95 monthly. FREE book on e-mail marketing.

Item	Description
Vendor	Gammadyne
Website	http://gammadyne.com/mmail.htm?ref=10088
Product Name	Mailer
Overview *(Based on verbiage from vendor Website)*	Gammadyne Mailer is an email automation utility. It can send personalized text or HTML email to a list of recipients located in a database or text file. It can also process virtually any type of incoming email, including bounce-backs, sign-ups, and opt-outs. Gammadyne Mailer's unmatched set of features includes multi-tasking, direct delivery, list-serving, auto-responding, auto-forwarding, command line support, exclusion lists, unlimited mailing list size, message preview, personalized attachments, duplicate elimination, and much more. Advanced list management features make it easy to add, change, verify, and remove recipients from the mailing list. For complex situations, you can use a powerful scripting language called G-Merge that has the versatility to automate even the most difficult of tasks. Good desktop solution for bulk e-mail handling. Doesn't include HTML editor or templates, but these can be found free elsewhere on the Web.
System Requirements	Works with all versions of Windows® 95, 98, NT, 2000, ME, XP, and 2003. Also, it should work on Virtual PC for the Mac version 6.01.
Price	**$149 for single-user license.**
Special Offers	FREE shareware version with restricted functionality. Purchase of full version includes FREE lifetime upgrades; no subscription fees.

Appendix 2 – Low-Priced E-Mail Newsletter List Management Software for Your PC

Item	Description
Vendor	Mach5 Enterprises
Website	http://www.mach5.com
Product Name	Mach5 Mailer
Overview *(Based on verbiage from vendor Website)*	Mach5 Mailer is like a Microsoft Word for e-mail. It merges the contents of your database to an e-mail message. It has advanced features that make creating exciting, targeted messages easy and fast. Handles newsletters, announcements, promotions, and update notices. HTML capability allows you to send combined HTML and plain text. HTML Import-from-web simplifies sending HTML messages. Desktop solution for bulk e-mail handling. Doesn't include HTML editor; only three newsletter templates.
System Requirements	Works with all versions of Windows® 98, ME, XP, and 2000.
Price	**$99.95 for single-user license.**
Special Offers	**FREE** shareware version with restricted functionality for 200 mailings or less. Purchase of full version includes **FREE** lifetime upgrades; no subscription fees.

Appendix 2 – Low-Priced E-Mail Newsletter List Management Software for Your PC

Item	Description
Vendor	MAPILab.com
Website	http://www.mapilab.com/outlook/
Product Name	Subscription Manager and Send Personally
Overview *(Based on verbiage from vendor Website)*	The Subscription Manager add-in (SUM) is designed for automatic adding/deleting subscribers to/from Microsoft Outlook 2000/XP distribution lists based on special e-mail messages from them (requests). Once a request is processed, SUM sends auto-reply with information about processing result. Auto-replies are created based on Outlook templates using special macros (expressions that are automatically replaced when sending a message). Add-in Send Personally (SPE) is designed to send messages to a great number of recipients via Microsoft Outlook. Add-in offers an alternative method of sending messages from Outlook, separate message being created for each recipient. The final recipient will get no information about the other recipients. Moreover, he/she will see only his/her name and address in the "To" field, as if the message was sent only to him/her. Certified Microsoft Outlook plug-ins to handle subscriptions, removals and personal e-mail issues associated with Outlook distribution lists. Limited functionality, but great productivity tools if you're just using Microsoft Word and Outlook to handle your newsletter.
System Requirements	• Microsoft Windows 95/NT4 or later • Microsoft Outlook 2000/XP/2003. • Can't work with Outlook 2000 when you use Microsoft Word as message editor. In this case you need use common Outlook message editor. • Works with all message editors in Outlook XP and Outlook 2003.
Price	**$24 each for single-user license.**
Special Offers	None.

Appendix 2 – Low-Priced E-Mail Newsletter List Management Software for Your PC

Item	Description
Vendor	AY Software Corporation
Website	http://www.aysoft.com/
Product Name	AY Mail 2.3 Professional
Overview *(Based on verbiage from vendor Website)*	AY Mail 2 Professional is designed for sophisticated users who send email messages to customers, clients or club members, run newsletters or highly targeted marketing campaigns. It allows you to process incoming mail on your existing mail account. AY Mail will extract all the automatic email messages, such as subscription and unsubscribe requests, bounces and read notifications, but will leave all your regular mail and manual responses from your contacts intact. If you don't have your own server this is the best way to handle responses (bounces, unsubscribes, etc.) to your mailings. Provides basic mail list management functionality and tracking at the desktop level. No HTML templates or editor.
System Requirements	• Microsoft Windows 95/NT4 or later • Microsoft Outlook 2000/XP/2003. • Can't work with Outlook 2000 when you use Microsoft Word as message editor. In this case you need use common Outlook message editor. • Works with all message editors in Outlook XP and Outlook 2003.
Price	**$139.95 for single-user license.**
Special Offers	None.

Appendix 2 – Low-Priced E-Mail Newsletter List Management Software for Your PC

Item	Description
Vendor	Desktop Server
Website	http://www.desktop-server.com/
Product Name	Desktop Server 4
Overview *(Based on verbiage from vendor Website)*	Instead of using the email server resources of your Internet service provider, Desktop Server 4 allows your personal PC to actually DO the bulk emailing. Desktop Server 4 will get your mail past more filters and IP blocks than any other bulk email software on the market. Designed to use your PC as a bulk e-mail instrument. If you have hundreds of clients, this would be a good package for you. No HTML templates or editor.
System Requirements	• PC with Window 95, 98, ME, IV, NT and XP. Or a Mac running Virtual PC. • You will need a PPP account (local service provider NOT AOL or CompuServe. • 32 megs of Ram • 1.6 Gig hard drive • Runs on any online service with Internet capability and port 25 available.
Price	**$299 for single-user license.**
Special Offers	None.

Item	Description
Vendor	Xequte
Website	http://www.xequte.com/maillistking/
Product Name	MailList King v.4.35
Overview *(Based on verbiage from vendor Website)*	With MailList King, you can create, manage and communicate with the people interested in your web site, products or organization. MailList King adds mailing list server functionality to Outlook and MAPI compliant e-mail software (Outlook Express, Eudora, Netscape, etc). Allowing users to opt-in subscribe, unsubscribe and send to your mailing list groups, with full support for personalization of messages, sending of acknowledgements and processing of undeliverable messages. Integrates with all popular e-mail software. Display of graphs and statistics on mailing list membership. Excellent list management solution for the price. Designed to work with Microsoft Outlook. No HTML templates or editor.
System Requirements	Windows 95/98/ME/NT/2000/XP
Price	**$49 for single-user license.**
Special Offers	None.

ABOUT THE AUTHOR

Al Kernek has been a licensed real estate broker in the state of California since 1978. He has previously owned and operated a real estate appraisal company and has been a mortgage broker as well. Al also has thirty years of executive-level marketing experience in both Fortune 500 firms and entrepreneurial start-up companies. He has extensive experience in Web marketing and the use of e-mail newsletters to promote products and services.

Among his many interests is a passion for bike riding along the California coastline, good mystery and horror novels, and charitable works. Al is a Toastmaster who resides with his wife and an assortment of critters in San Diego, California.

INDEX

Index

Microsoft Outlook Contact file, 31, 36, 55
  Subscription Manager, 123
Microsoft Word, 2, 3, 4, 5, 14, 16, 31, 36, 37, 39, 40, 41, 42, 43, 44, 45, 46, 52, 53, 54, 60, 75, 84, 85, 89, 90, 91, 114, 122, 123, 124
Outsource Services, 1, 2, 64, 65, 66, 67, 86, 87, 90, 92, 93, 97, 99, 100
  Newsletter, 67
PDF, 26, 41, 45, 53, 67
Plans
  Action, 92, 93
  Strategy 83, 84, 85, 86, 87, 88, 89, 91, 92, 93, 96, 97, 99
Self Assessment Survey, 83, 90, 91, 92, 93
Tips, 6, 43, 81
Web Authoring, 60, 61, 62, 77, 88, 89, 91, 97, 102, 107
  Software
    Easy Web Editor, 103
    High Impact eMail 2.0, 104
    Publisher 2003, 105
    SiteSpinner, 106
    Web Author with Image Mapper, 107
    Web Studio, 112
    WebEasy, 109
    WebEditor6, 110
    WebExpress, 111
    Webpage Creation Kit, 108
Web Hosting, 20, 57, 74, 75, 76, 77, 90, 106
  Vendors 78
Web Layout, 40
  Search engines, 81, 82
Web Software
  BlueLark, 80
Website, 72